Praise for *How Time Moves:*

"Those familiar with Caryn Mirriam-Goldberg's verse know the humor, the inventiveness, and the revelations. Her *How Time Moves: New and Selected Poems* samples generously from all of her books, a span of twenty-five years. The new poems show a master poet at work, as in 'Thresholds,' where story and song blend to create a further dimension, where 'all the gears of blossom / keep turning, all the doors continually open wide.' Like William Blake's 'doors of perception,' these pages lead readers inward and outward at once. Congratulations to her for this stupendous book!"
 ~ Denise Low, 2007-09 Kansas Poet Laureate, *Shadow Light: Poems,* Red Mountain Press Editor's Award

"This poet testifies her tug of kinship to feral storms, kitchen appliances, crows, the pluck of old ladies, helpless love, and other denizens of the wide world brought living to her pages. Drawn from twenty five years of lyric devotion, Caryn brings this harvest to Meadowlark Books in a collection with gifts for everyone: blessing, consolation, self-portrait, field guide, yoga gesture, biblical telling, song, memory, spell. She is our teacher speaking from the sky, from the field, from the heartland."
 ~ Kim Stafford, Oregon Poet Laureate & author of *Wild Honey, Tough Salt*

"Caryn Mirriam-Goldberg is a generous and insightful poet, brave in her candor and ever awake to the world around her, ready for all the truth it can offer her each day. In Mirriam-Goldberg's poetry, even cancer becomes epiphany, an occasion of ecstatic awakening. This is the real work of a poet—to see and speak the often-hidden truths of a human life in a way that enlightens and informs. In the cumulative power of her new and selected poems, Caryn Mirriam-Goldberg accomplishes this with grace, insight, courage, and unceasing wonder."
 ~ Patricia Traxler, author of *Naming the Fires*

"Caryn Mirriam-Goldberg's *How Time Moves* enacts the largesse and endurance of the upright piano on its cover, in poems that span a life with "the urgency of living in a world on the cusp of vanishing." True to its title, time is a paramount issue in these poems—not simply its passing, but its potential, in complicity with imagination, to invent and resurrect the future. 'From years ahead, I wait for her to turn into the future,' she writes of her great-grandmother in a Lithuanian village whose inhabitants 'will face the gun or the gas chamber," ". . . and the breath / from her body that will one day be my body.' The poems extend over the decades of Mirriam-Goldberg's extraordinary life, from her childhood in Brooklyn, 'where my fingernails formed in utero,' to the Kansas prairie. The bridge between past and future is 'a freeway of stars,' and wind, and breath, and always, for Caryn Mirriam-Goldberg, poetry."

~ Diane Seuss, author of *Four-Legged Girl* and *Still Life with Two Dead Peacocks and a Girl*

"In *How Time Moves*, Caryn Mirriam-Goldberg offers us a magical gift: a compilation of new and selected poems, rich with memory and meaning. 'Expect to be startled,' the poet tells us. And we are. Mirriam-Goldberg's distinctive voice is a steadying hand on the shoulder, as she gently steers us through her treasured Kansas landscape, or turns our gaze toward the faces of her beloveds. The poet reminds us that 'the holy does not play by our rules,' then deftly proceeds to make all things holy: her prayers tucked into Ponderosa pines, cranes who stencil the sky, clouds of tilted silver, the lingering touch of a lover or child. Through her brilliant mastery of craft and ever-present compassion, Mirriam-Goldberg offers us a wise, humorous, breathtakingly diverse glimpse into her world—as well as the world of our shared human experience. As the poet tenderly says: 'I want to know this song that breaks the mouths / of humans.' Her own song is one of piercing honesty and exuberant hope, a rare voice in a fractured world. *How Time Moves* lingers long in the heart and mind, an enduring reminder of the deep and lasting power of poetry.'

~ Joy Roulier Sawyer, author of *Lifeguards* and *Tongues of Men and Angels*

"Caryn Mirriam-Goldberg admonishes us: 'All the songs you love will return like an old cat. // Expect to be startled.' Believe her. *How Time Moves* is the glimmering songbook of her poetic oeuvre—a single vol-

ume containing a book's worth of new work in four chapters along with choice excerpts from each of her previous six poetry volumes. Here, time becomes both particle ('. . . the brown bricks chipped / by time and the stress of lasting') and wave: ('The friend you love is all ashes now / waiting for you and others to scatter. // The ideas you have about time or what's right / are lighter than all that ash.') Amidst the tumult of time's flow, there are also introspective interludes: 'Place a wintered leaf / of your old thoughts / on a flat rock. Wait. // Watch what the pine, an arrow / of desire for the sun, does with time . . .' It is the universality of time's passage joined with the specificity and intimacy Mirriam-Goldberg uses to illumine and delineate her own times that make this a rare book to cherish, a consummate gift of grace.'
~ Roy Beckemeyer, author of *Mouth Brimming Over*

"For Caryn Mirriam-Goldberg, witnessing often means 'dwelling in what we don't know.' *How Time Moves*, her stellar new omnibus, allows us to witness a world redolent of possibility, a half-known world in which we can fling ourselves across the dewy air to discover we can fly. Caryn writes, 'to be awake enough in any place is . . . to hear what sings beneath the human-made world.' Layer upon layer of this book houses new and sometimes familiar friends who find each other in the cleansing light of the wind. And if this new collection is indeed a type of house, it is surely a great tree that sings boldly from below our human doings, 'Its arms holding up rooms full of birds.'"
~ Tyler Robert Sheldon, Editor-in-Chief of *MockingHeart Review* and author of *Driving Together*

Praise for previous collections of poetry:

"The poems are as close to prayer as language can get, if prayer is vision that sees into the souls of things and music that makes us move to old healing rhythms. I find myself writing whole stanzas in my journal and quoting phrases to friends wondering, 'Now who said that?' She gives voice to what can't be put into words, sets us free of old paradigms, and writes like a dream."
~ Julia Alvarez, author of *In the Time of Butterflies*

"'Nothing prepares you for the real,' writes Caryn Mirriam-Goldberg in the soaring flock of tones and images that is this wonderful book of poems. Nothing prepares us, and so we stumble and fall and break into blossom, bite persimmons, and birth ourselves again and again. How any of us weather the darkening climate of these times is a wonder; it is such books as this that help us breathe."
    ~ David Abram, author, *The Spell of the Sensuous*

"Mirriam-Goldberg is a master of the paradoxical as she gifts the reader with insights that are at once disconcerting and comforting; as she holds joy and grief in the same hand, and asks us to trust the maker of these poems—her courage, her wisdom, and her truthtelling, as if she's lived infinity."
    ~ Maureen Seaton, author of *Cave of the Yellow Volkswagen* and *Sex Talks to Girls*

"The poems are silver threads that weave through the darkening sky and gates and light unspooling from the heart's loom a dream of joy and ancestral echoes."
    ~ Jimmy Santiago Baca, author, *A Glass Of Water* and *Singing At The Gates*. Founder, Cedar Tree, Inc.

"Caryn Mirriam-Goldberg's voice is imbued with love, humor, and wisdom. She wields plain words powerfully. Her comprehension of nature borders on the absolute. Her wonderful poems state the seamlessness of the cosmic and mundane, the molten paradoxes of intimacy and otherness, identity and separation."
    ~ Stephanie Mills, author, *Epicurian Simplicity* and *In Service of the Wild*.

"Caryn Mirriam-Goldberg is a wise, witty, and wry poet."
    ~ Alicia Ostriker, author of *The Little Space: Poems Selected and New*

"These noble, ecstatic poems reflect a woman on the edge of life and death. She runs like any animal into the dark 'that isn't so dark' and with new eyes sees there what sustains her—a different light, a hidden room, hope and healing. Her words capture the richness of Kansas landscape and the internal wildness of animals that feed our very existence, give us courage to breathe in every minute and move on."

~ Perie Longo, author, *The Privacy of Wind*

"*Animals in the House* is a collection of poems that celebrates the power of the natural world to shape us into what we're meant to be. These poems lift us out of the container we call our selves, shape us toward trusting what we can never completely know, place us more firmly on the trustworthy ground of earth that has the power to heal and renew. These poems tell us what matters is what's up close and they make what matters close in case we've forgotten. Caryn Mirriam-Goldberg walks through the fire—of her longing, her childhood, her desire, her hauntings—all senses pried open, through 'a dark that isn't so dark' into a light that 'dissolves borders into bluestem.'"

~ Renee Gregorio, author, *The Storm That Tames Us*

"'The earth is tilting,' Caryn Mirriam-Goldberg writes, offering us unexpected, empowering angles from which to reconsider our traditions."

~ Diane Wolkstein, author of *Inanna: Queen of Heaven*

"There were never two women, just Caryn Mirriam-Goldberg split into myths, riper than pomegranates and out of all time. I love these poems."

~ Stanley Lombardo, translator of *The Illiad*

How Time Moves
New and Selected Poems

Meadowlark Press, LLC
meadowlark-books.com
PO Box 333
Emporia, KS 66801

Copyright © 2020 Caryn Mirriam-Goldberg
www.CarynMirriamGoldberg.com

Cover Photo & *How Time Moves* division page photos by Tony Peterson.
Author Photo by Dave Leiker.

All rights reserved.

ISBN: 978-1-7342477-2-5

Library of Congress Control Number: 2020932865

How Time Moves
New and Selected Poems

Caryn Mirriam-Goldberg

Meadowlark Press, LLC
Emporia, Kansas

Selected Books

Poetry

Following the Curve

Chasing Weather: Tornadoes, Tempests, and Thunderous Skies in Word & Image, with photographer Stephen Locke

Landed

Animals in the House

Reading the Body

Lot's Wife

Fiction

Miriam's Well

The Divorce Girl

Non-Fiction

Everyday Magic: A Field Guide to the Mundane and Miraculous

Poem on the Range: A Poet Laureate's Love Song to Kansas

Needle in the Bone: How a Holocaust Survivor and Polish Resistance Fighter Beat the Odds and Found Each Other

The Sky Begin At Your Feet: A Memoir on Cancer, Community and Coming Home to the Body

Anthologies Edited

Transformative Language Arts in Action, co-edited with Ruth Farmer

To the Stars Through Difficulties: A Kansas Renga in 150 Voices

The World Keeps Turning Toward Light: A Renga from the State Poets Laureate of America

Begin Again: 150 Kansas Poems

An Endless Skyway: Poems from the State Poets Laureate of America, co-edited with Walter Bargen, Denise Low & Marilyn K. Taylor

The Power of Words: A Transformative Language Arts Anthology, co-edited with Janet Tallman

For Ken

Table of Contents

Introduction 1

❖ How Time Moves ❖

Inscription 7

Time Travel

Crossing Over 11
The Thread 12
God in the Trees 13
Riding Backwards Through Childhood 14
When the Train Stops in Brooklyn 15
Visitor 16
The First Man You Loved 17
The Gone Ones 18
Where Have You Gone? 19
How to See 20
When I Was Half My Age 21
August First 22
Valentine 24
In Transit 25
How Time Moves 26

Time Names its Age

When We Were Kestrels 29
So Much Could Be Other Than It Is 30
Copeland Falls 31
The Sound of the Big Thompson 32
Under the 400-Year-Old Ponderosa Pine 33
The Fire Says 34
The Language of Art 35

The People Who Pose in Front of Monet's Water Lilies 36
Talking to William Stafford Late at Night 37
The Last Light of the Year 38
The Coldest Night 39
The Rain Returns 40
Prevernal 41
Almost Gone 42
Time Names Its Age 43

Pandemic Time

Pandemic Time 47
We Have Prepared For This All Our Lives 49
Is It Spring? Is It Winter? 51
Pandemic Travel 52
Last Night, I Dreamt of Mount Etna 53
The Night John Prine Died 54
I Don't Know How to Love the Broken Day 55
This Summer 56
Your Grief For What You've Lost 57
To My Great-Grandmother Who Died in One Pandemic
From Her Great-Granddaughter Alive in Another 58
A Year From Now 61
What Is a Year? 62
Who Is At the Door Now? 63
Where Is the Answer? 64
Havdalah 65
There Is a Door 66

Everything that Rises

No One Tells You What to Expect 69
Who Dances? 70
Surprise Lilies 72
Stone, Star, Field 73
Thresholds 76
All Those Birds Flying Off That Tree 77
The Fight 78
What Happens in the Dark 79
All I Have Lost to February 80

After the Winter of No Winter 81
Mystery Street 82
What You Need is Here..83
Permission 84
This is Not the Easy Poem to Write 85
I Will Not Be Afraid of Women 86
Everything That Rises..87

Gateway

When the Moon Opened My Life 91
What the Mostly Blind Eye Sees..92
The Wish 93
In the Middle of Cancer 94
Teaching the White Fire..95
The Opposite of Certainty 97
The Sound of Crickets Slowed to Human Time 99
No Other Way 100
When the Sun is Closest to the Earth..101
Shabbat 102
The Midrash of the Heart..103
Jericho 104
My Road Worth Walking Down..105
You Are Never Alone 106
Gateway..107

❖ Following the Curve ❖

Following the Curve..115
Getting Started..116
Healing 117
Child's Pose (Balasana) 118
Am I My Feet? 119
Downward-Facing Dog (Adho Mukha Svanasana) 120
I Love This Body That's Not the Way I Thought....................................121
Mountain (Tadasana)..122
In the Middle of the Yoga Studio 123
The Dead Poet's Yoga Class 124
Sun Salutation (Suyra Namaska)..126

The Yoga of Memory..127
Finding the Fire (Tapas) 128
Warrior II (Virabhadrasana II) 129
Body of Time 130
Triangle (Trikonasana)...131
The Yoga of Injustice, Betrayal, and Anxiety................................132
Self-Study (Svadhyaya)...133
Tree (Vrksasana) 134
The Yoga of Trees 135
Balancing on the Equinox 136
Half Moon (Arch Chandrasana)...137
What the Ocean Can Know of a Body 138
Find Your Seat (Utkatanasa)..140
The Yoga of Old Wounds 141
Devotion (Ishvara Pranidhara)...142
Prayer Twist (Namaska Parsvakonasana).....................................143
Let the Body Speak..144
The Dharma of the Arms 145
Forearm Plank (Makara Adho Mukha Svanasana).....................146
Headstand (Sirsasana) 147
I Sing to My Bones..148
The Yoga of Forgiveness 149
Yoga Class Overlooking Four Oxen, Three Cars,
Two Pick-Up Trucks, and One Blue Heron 151
The Yoga of Sex 152
The Holy...153
Corpse Pose (Savasana) at the End of Yoga Class 154
Contentment (Santos) 155
Your Body is a Conversation With the World............................156

❖ Chasing Weather ❖

Welcome 159
Panorama...160
Respect the Storm of the Storm..161
Goodnight, Texas...162
What the Sky is Made Of 163
The Light In Between...164
Supercell 165

Finding the Moon	166
The Bridge	167
What Do You Believe In?	168
Celebrate This Kansas	169
What Would Happen If You Walked Here?	170
Dead End	171
Convergence	172
Seeing in the Dark	173
The Woman Who Watches the Sky	174
Where the Road Ends	175
After the Storm, the Stars	176
You Rise Up To Meet the Falling World	177
Finding the Question	178
Your Road	179
All Night at the Truck Stop	180
Beginner	181
Being Made of Weather	182
When the Brokenness Vanishes Before Your Eyes	183
Not Rare But Precious	184
When the Rain Comes	185
Field Love	186
Mercy. Daring. Courage.	187
Coordinates	188
Questions For Home	189
Chasing Weather	190
Entering the Days of Awe	191
Rain	192
Surrender	193
Return	194
Late Night in June	195
Imagine You Know How to Fly	196
Do You Know Where You're From?	197
Blue	198
The Door of the Grass	199
In Gratitude	200
Whoever You Are, Come Back	201
Light	202
Interlude	203
Climate Is What You Expect, Weather Is What You Get	204

Flight Plan 205
Two Bodies Always In Motion 206
Love Dissolves Your Name 207
Prayer For a New Year 208

❖ Landed ❖

Joy 211
Winter Solstice: 4:22 p.m. 212
The Photographer 213
Borderline 214
Migration of Animals 215
Lost 216
Lullaby for the Changing Moon 217
My Daughter Six Years Before Her Birth 218
What Isn't a Prayer Anymore? 219
After Woody Went Back to the Forest 220
Just-Doing-That-Moon 221
What Isn't Possible? 222
Advice for the Material World 223
Nouns I Have Loved 224
The Life You Could Be Living (If You Weren't Living This One) ... 225
Billboards 226
The Dreaming Land 227
Self-Portrait as River of Starlings 228
Self-Portrait Before Birth 229
Self-Portrait at Two and a Half 230
Self-Portrait at Nine 231
Self-Portrait as Oldest Child 232
Self-Portrait as Grown-Up 233
Self-Portrait at Twenty-Five 234
Self-Portrait as Pond 235
Self-Portrait at Forty-Two 236
Self-Portrait as Bodhisattva 237
Self-Portrait as Fuckhead 237
Self-Portrait as KitchenAid Mixer 238

Self-Portrait as Hand	239
Self-Portrait as Ecstasy	240
Self-Portrait for Day-Long Life	241
Self-Portrait at Sixty	242
Self-Portrait as Insomnia	243
Self-Portrait at Eighty	244
Self-Portrait as Woman Who Loves Her Body for a Moment	245
Self-Portrait as Wind	246
Jubilee	247
The Road is Just a River	248
Five-Year Anniversary at the Grand Canyon	249
That Tree is a Genius	250
I Would Touch You	251
Alive	252
In the End, There is Only Kindness	253
Daniel's Dream Speaks	254
Prayer for the Moment of Change	255
Your Heart Has No Gate	256
Landed	257
The Last Moment	258

❖ Reading the Body ❖

Discovering Fire	261
Diagnosis	262
Morning Glory	263
The Landscape of the Body	264
Already	265
Lilac	266
What Do You Want to Remember?	267
Breastless	268
Your Life is Your Life	270
I Want To Tell You How Beautiful You Are	271
Reading the Body	272
Playing the Cello	273
Bridges	274

❖ Animals in the House ❖

Girl 277
Magnolia Tree in Kansas 278
Tricks of Gravity 279
About Desire 280
Leap 282
What I Could Tell 283
Happiness 284
The Wishing Tree Talks 286
Almost Totality: Partial Eclipse 287
The Dark Between the Stars 288
Three Walking Songs for the Night 290
Lightning, No Thunder 292
Burning the Prairie 293
Telling My Son About His Birth 295
Jonah and the Tree 296
Swimming in Mombasa at Midnight 297
Hills Climb the Sky 298
What the Earth Holds 299
Holly 300
The Speed of Life 302
Animals in the House 303
Spring Song 307

❖ Lot's Wife ❖

The Mortician's Daughter 311
Imaginary Friend 312
The Bad Monster Contemplates Her Badness
from a Lounge Chair in K-Mart 314
Hagar on the Mountain 315
Rapunzel in the Desert 316
The Snow Queen 317
The Woman Who Cannot Feel 318
Three Women with Breast Cancer 319
Inside the Wolf 320
Psyche 321
Circe Bawls Out An Aging Snow White 322

Lazarus's Wife 323
The Woman Who Saved Moses 324
Demeter is Persephone 325
Song of Songs 326
Lot's Wife 328
The Grandmother in the Mental Hospital 329
Eve in Northwestern Australia 331
Eurydice 332
Moses's Sister 333
Leah 334
Cinderella's Mother as Hazel Tree 335
Mirrors 336
Telling My Daughter About Her Birth 338
I Love You 339

Acknowledgments 343
Source Notes 344
Publication Acknowledgments 345
About the Photographer 350
About the Author 351

Introduction: I Write in the Field

I write in the field, a grassy slope of half-brome, half-native prairie, surrounded by hills of Osage orange and cedar woods. Whenever possible, I write on the screened-in porch, immersed in wind, which is the way of the world here. When it's too cold to be outside, I sit in a chair before three south-facing windows, looking up from my laptop toward the dozen hues of tan and rust across the land and the startling deep blue of sky that create winter. But it is always the field that surrounds me, that I remember when I'm apart from it, that teaches me the most about how to write and live.

In the field, I hear the rhythms that climb and run, fall and sleep: cicadas and crickets overflowing the banks of summer, the ever-present punctuation of blue jays doing their squeaky swing call all spring, the crows cawing me back to the sky come fall and the winter flock clustering around the feeder in the cold. I let go of finding the words long enough to find the world. All I need to know about poetry is right here. Just listen. Just stop.

My poetics is best described by poet Li-Young Lee who, once said, "The whole Universe is humming, is vibrating. It's that hum that I want to hear. That's the subject of my poems . . . The words are like birds that perch on this frequency of sound." Since I started writing poetry when I was fourteen, it has always been this humming, this vibration, this frequency of sound that draws me to the page. The words drop in to hold up the power lines of the rhythm, which carries forth the voice of the poem, the essay, the story.

The humming is everywhere, those rhythms of one place or another unfolding where and who we truly are. Of course, we don't just inhabit place: we live in time, a human construct of how we order the world as well as the ecological ground of how seasons shift, weather migrates, and the cycles of birth, age, death, and renewal unfurl. I used to think I was primarily writing about place until it occurred to me that my poetry constantly grapples with what time is and how it moves. Like all of us, I live in the place called time, and that place—a field within the field—is dizzyingly diverse and deep, made of stories and histories, callings and yearnings, hard-won wisdom and pure mystery. What does it mean to live in time? I circle around the fire of that question through my poems, gravitating toward what light and heat I glimpse.

Being awake enough in one particular place and time lets fall away the noise of the human-made world to reveal what sings beyond, beneath, and around our ideas and habits. But, of course, what place, just like what muse, resonates for one person may not touch another. It took me a while to find mine.

Growing up in Brooklyn, NY, and central New Jersey, I rarely felt at home. I would stare at trees through an apartment window or, years later, walk past the bounds of our housing development, and pace along corn fields, making up poems in my head. I dreamed of living far away, and my Polish grandfather, who immigrated here as a child, told me that when I was very young, I said I was going to live in Kansas when I grew up. In my early twenties, I discovered not just Kansas in general but this field in particular—this land that had been in my husband's family for five generations. Immediately, I wanted to be here, where we've built a home, made a family, crafted our livelihoods, and wandered through a lot of different weather of heartbreak, joy, illness, courage, grief, and homecoming.

Now that I've been a Midwesterner longer than I was an Easterner, I'm finally starting to see more clearly the patterns that sift through the land, season by season. I'm in relationship with particulars here—butterfly milkweed, big bluestem, deer birthing season, spider migrations, thunderstorm season. I wake up in the morning and always go first to the windows to see what crows call out their domain over our compost pile, what deer linger along the woods or walk slowly near the kids' swing set. I go to sleep at night staring at Orion through the window while coyotes fight each other on the hill or owls call in a broken harmonic.

In the summer nights, I walk out to the herb garden to watch lightning bugs in the grasses even if it means I'll have to shower right away to knock off quick chiggers. In the fall, I watch the sumac glowing red in the rain. In the spring, there's the redbud that's never red and the slip of bobcat or bluebird in the nearby woods if I look at the right place at the right time. Here's what tends my words, in the middle of a field, in the middle of the continent, and somewhat past the middle of my life.

Writing in the field is a calling with two hearts for me: I also write in the field of Transformative Language Arts, an emerging discipline I helped start over twenty years ago, or more accurately, gave another name to an ancient human impulse to make something of meaning out of words and share it for the good for all. I always loved the sky, breeze, oranging of the horizon, and indigo bunting bursting iridescent blue across the sky, and I remember always wanting to create something—a drawing, a poem, a song—from the flood of impulses these signs of the living earth unleashed in me. But it wasn't until I was in my mid-twenties that I found teaching (more accurately, facilitating—holding the brave space where people can find their own truths) was part of my life's work. Just like with writing, facilitating others arriving at their words and what's beyond is all about opening our peripheral vision more to see what's already here, then making something to bring us more meaning, vitality, and joy.

My writing workshops, coaching sessions, consultations, and classes with people often focus on coming together in a time and place—a commons—where simply by listening to ourselves and each other, we make miracles. For those being witnessed, there's a powerful sense of being heard that often allows them to connect with a wider perspective of their lived stories and future possibilities. For those witnessing, there's freedom found in the infinite width of weather and change, the wild depths of love and courage.

There is something analogous about witnessing one another and witnessing the earth through writing. Both require surrendering where our minds usually swim, drown, or flood. Both call for a certain suspension of disbelief—putting aside everyday judgments, opinions, and well-worn stories we tell ourselves of who, what, and where we are supposed to be. Instead, we come together and just listen to what rises up and comes to the page, the room, the field we inhabit together. We come home to ourselves to feel the wind that rises and falls, the more-than-humans among us that drop their leaves or pick up the fallen berries.

But writing and witnessing means dwelling in what we don't know. Sitting on the earth and trying to contemplate the mysteries inherent in a square inch of dirt could take a lifetime. The same is true for a square inch of our lives. Listening to another means learning the new language of this specific time and place. So I keep learning how to tune into the collective humming of place in the local wind spurring the birds higher over the field until, along with our words, they land on power lines running through this time.

Caryn Mirriam-Goldberg

How Time Moves
New and Selected Poems

Caryn Mirriam-Goldberg

Inscription

How does the world tell our story?
A line of one cloud overlaps another.
An airplane gone but for its tail.
A first star barely inscribed on evening
before the page turns dark.

What does the first reddening leaf sing down its veins
to loosen the grip of twig from branch?
How does the cricket know to comb its wings
into the rhythm of August ending?

In the middle of a life, what tells us to turn quickly
from the oncoming car or edge of a nightmare
before dropping down to safety again?

What speaks through us at the cusp of winter,
the heavy hands of the next day's humidity,
or the last magnolia bud not ruined by last night's frost
knocked off the tree by a speeding squirrel?

Look away from the words composing the mind
into the blank sky, not quite gray, not quite blue,
that dissolves into the wind of the world.

Time Travel

Crossing Over

At the edge of the yard somewhere in Lithuania,
she takes it all in: the white bark of the forest,
the dark vertical shadows, the tall field between here
and horizon. Wind rises from the banks
of trees and rushes everywhere, reminding her
to lift her chest, inhale sharply, remember.

Who will come after her, and then what?
Will the grasses part the same way in tomorrow's weather,
the leaves sing their breaking song, the air hold
the weight of the world evenly around each being?
Is she the first or the last to hear the ending world?

From years ahead, I wait for her to turn into the future.
When she does, her face catches the late light,
and she sees me, sitting cross-legged on a wooden floor
in Kansas. What is there to say from there to here
that would help? A cow walks through a parking lot,
a peacock screams, all of us far from oceans, wars,
the urgency of living in a world on the cusp of vanishing.

My great-grandmother doesn't know she will die
in that very spot facing away from soldiers and fire.
How most of this village will face the gun or the gas chamber,
quickly or slowly in the camps or holes in the ground,
little space to think the best, last thought.
The air she exhales falls off the earth, like the sun
tonight and every night. Her surviving children
will spread like water on hard ground that softens over time,
so far from her view at the edge of the yard.

All she knows is the cleansing light of the wind,
the moment her life balances before her,
the way love can shelter itself as a dark bird not-so-hidden
in the birches, ready to exhale from the leaves
that keep remaking themselves and the breath
from her body that will one day be my body.

The Thread

My mother singing "Tora Lora Lora,"
an Irish lullaby although we were Brooklyn Jews.
The vacuum's roar muffled by shag carpeting
while the birch banged on the hapless window sill.
The humming refrigerator in the middle of the night
when everyone slept or paced alone in the old house.
The chants encasing me in each swaying note
as I wrapped my thin arms around my cold chest
in the cavernous synagogue. The creak of the swing
as I turned horizontal, defying gravity in the static
of the transistor radio. The old staccato of my father's anger.
The loud slap on the bass notes of the bare torso
making new bruises, then the slow breath pacing in
until the danger was gone. All the possibilities in each
novel about a girl born afraid but about to enter the calm pond
of my life and swim. Bike tires on wet pavement at dawn.
The first kiss in the back of the school bus broken by applause.
How rain parts its pouring for thunder's interior roar.
The mornings revved up like motorcycles, the exhaling speed
of rivers, starving for new ground or betrayed by rocks
toward the remembering willows, singing reed by reed.
The happy rhythm of the subway rocking my spine
in and out of alignment with the dark, tunneling through water,
all the buzzing bodies ferrying millions of cells into sound,
the miracle of one rushing animal carrying us all.

God in the Trees

First god was in the trees.
Don't ask me how I knew. I just did.
The tree would shake. I would shiver.

Where I grew up, we measured our days
in highway exits, the seconds of breath
to hold in the flashing intervals of a tunnel.
But I fell in love with trees anyway.

Sometimes the tree would blow against the window
of the synagogue, and I would shiver again.
A good coincidence, I told myself, for this to happen
in what they told me was the house of god

although I knew the house was a tree,
its legs flourishing downward into secret roots
that drank from underground rivers rushing slow,
its arms holding up rooms full of birds

shivering just like me as I watched the tree also
from my bedroom window in Brooklyn
or stood beneath it while I was supposed to be
walking to school, touching the bark, asking,
in the chill that touched my spine, god not to leave me:

the open canopy of leaf or bare branch to wrap
around me like a prayer, the words of god
blowing through me without words.

Riding Backwards Through Childhood

Start on the freeway, its asphalt black with promise,
the long stretches of refineries and factories,
the brown pockets of water where seabirds die slowly.
Necessary, your parents tell you before you arrive
at the next house made of new wood and fresh paint,
pale green siding that will never die, and a milk box
that doubles as a refrigerator in the blizzard of '68.
New trees park in front of each house, eager to reach
across the street in a canopy of reunion years from now.

You ride further: the brownstones hold onto each other
like complacent sisters. There's yours: a stained glass sailboat
in the window beside the front door. Your father
parks the Buick in the driveway so you and your brother
can take turns aiming the hoses toward the car again,
although you're more interested in soaking each other,
even if it means getting spanked and sent inside,
worth it all to hold the power of rivers.

Now rush along the elevated tracks into
the squares of sky between apartments that aren't
yours until one is: the brown bricks chipped
by time and the stress of lasting. Your mother,
crying or just finished, looks at nothing
through the window. Something burns in the oven.
Your father is around the corner, playing poker,
cheating just a little. Part of how he earns a living,
he'll say later, which is earlier.

Then the peach rose spiraling into curved petals.
You reach to put it in your mouth, where words don't yet live.
It rains. A squirrel runs toward you. You don't know anything
but winter, the season of your birth, with its blue
glass, blue sky, blue rain, until you're far enough back
that there is no ride, no you, no fleck of desperation
to begin, no speed or weight, just a freeway of stars
and darkness that holds more stars and darkness.

Caryn Mirriam-Goldberg

When the Train Stops in Brooklyn

The conductor doesn't know how long we'll be here,
can't tell us why we're paused, the doors of time open,
to let in the merciful wind and my childhood
neighborhood banked in orange light.

This is where my fingernails formed in utero,
my heart came into beating, my arms learned to unfurl.
Where I first saw this sky, early December
snowless days and moonless nights.

Look, say the seagulls with their wingtips,
this is where green tinsel bannered the streets together
while I lay in the back of the station wagon,
all that shine swimming over me.

Where my mother sang along with Barbra
while vacuuming, her young face blushing petal
and pain in her loneliness while I played
Red Light Green Light 123, the tree sturdy
as the house wasn't, while all the houses around
claimed their territory in Yiddish or Spanish.
This is where the now-dead argued over urgent bills,
and the now-living made coffee while remembering
where they were a year or a decade ago.

The doors close, the conductor announces motion
stories above stories, strangers crossing below
and between rows of scalloped brick tops, blue awnings,
racing diagonals of a thousand fire escapes
mimicking the danger and possibility of every step
into the clickety-clack future.

Visitor

for Ravi

"Come, I will teach you," your young self
tells my young self in the school gymnasium.
I learn how to step wide while turning
with such speed that I can spin around your step.

You already know that you will never go back
to your country, just as I must live a half continent
away from where I started. How long
have we known each other?

In the dream, you show me a photo of your son, not yet born,
and place a few small stones on the grave of my father
long before he died. I call you on the phone in my sleep,
forgetting we are not the same person.

Sometimes when you wake, you reach for my glasses
only to find your own. The music changes, but not time:
we are still practicing in the empty university classroom
or turning up the cassette player in the parking lot,

decades later from when we started. Like a dust devil
on the hot black surface so open and bare, we whirl crooked,
a Jew and a Tamil dancing the Swedish hambo.
Each step a leap around you, your brown arms light
as fallen leaves. I hold on and fly.

The First Man You Loved

He crossed one thin leg tightly over the other,
leaned to light a cigarette of the recent past
with the fire of the future. Your grandfather
holding you on his lap so you could stare in stereo
across the park to the big kids kicking a deflating ball
into the present, just missing your head.

It's 45 years after your grandfather died,
one hand holding a new pack of cigarettes,
his other hand on the door handle of his store.
The sky is unusually pink this December morning
at the end of another decade. An envelope
on your desk holds new old photos of the others—
your grandmother, father, whole sheaves of uncles,
people you can't remember from college,
even the ones you swore to love across streets
of change long before you understood what endures.

The first man who ever loved you didn't say much.
You sat on his lap, dunking your cookie in his tea,
both of you lost in the black and white flashes
of a showdown at the O.K. Corral, sunset
reddening the rectangles of time we call windows.
He let you be, which was how you knew what love was.

The Gone Ones

for Lauren

I slap down a photo of Grandma, one hand on her hip,
the other around a palm tree, her face daring the future,
which slapped back. Lauren shows me Grandma
on a park bench, pigeons at her feet, and amazingly,
one against her left cheek, both of us sorting pictures
at high speed for our children, brother and sister, selves.

We find our grandfather holding the son who died
before our mother was born, our grandmother's sisters
in their weighted Victorian dresses years before
the Holocaust erased them, a crowd of dead cousins
so alive at a restaurant in Brooklyn in the 1940s,
each man's tie matched to his wife's corsage,
each wife's bangs curled above her Cleopatra eyes.

We sort our children, laughing in kitchen sinks
where they have their baths, or unduly concerned
as we carry them in their carseats home from birth.
We find old boyfriends, new couches long ago hauled
to dumpsters, and wedding kisses of couples now divorced.

The trash pile grows: double prints of double prints,
off-focus rectangles of sand dunes or red rock, people
we don't know anymore or never did, and the terrier
I held against my flat chest before he followed Lauren
across the street as she was following me, no way
of knowing the trash truck was rounding the corner.
Then the polaroid shots, blurred, but still the rainbow
over our house the day our infant brother died.

We find people dancing who swore they never danced,
birthday cakes, palm trees and sunglasses, strangers
kissing our then-skinny grandmother at the beach,
and familiar smiles wearing the clothes we wore
so long ago, staring happily or wearily into the future
as if to say, *Oh, there you are. I was waiting.*

Where Have You Gone?

for Jerry

Where have you gone, my little friend,
quiet in the corner of the couch, or standing
to hold me, your heart beating through mine?

Where are you hidden or hiding just now,
four months afterwards, three years later?
Are you closer or farther or nowhere at all?
Is your absence a chickadee feather
in the paper litter of leaves or a raindrop
dissolving the gravel of the driveway?
Is the weather pleasant, the company entertaining,
the music a polka or waltz played on accordion?

Are you happy and out of pain?
Do you miss us, or is your mind more
like the space framed between cedar spires?
Can you fly or is the question irrelevant?

How did you go from that hospital bed, old pal?
A leaf detaching, a deer dissolving into fog,
a branch bending with no apparent breeze
or weight of bird. A trick of faith
erasing you from our lives?

How To See

You think the way you see is a commons,
right in the middle of a Midwestern college town
where all the regular Joes mill about, calling out
"Daffodil!", "Blue bench!", "Red coffee mug still warm!"

You think we all see the same stream, to the left
winding through moss where someone planted
one jonquil in 1967, now turned into a thousand,
and to the right, a freshly-built housing complex
with matching faux balconies and red trim.

On the cobblestone plaza someone laid 100 years ago,
you think you see nothing but the yellow wrapper
of a cough drop, and later, someone's three-year-old,
squatted low, reaching out to catch what he can't
of falling cottonwood fluff before it turns to snow.

You don't remember learning to see in the womb,
a pale shadow of someone approaching
or the tight space between where your mother ends
and the car dashboard begins, until the violent
disruption of light that doesn't soften, only sharpens
until you are old, looking away from the crowd
at the leggy creek where water winds over rock.

None or all of what you see is you: the tendrils
of earth and all its DNA in its variety pack of spirals
winding through time. Or is it time exhaling
into another blossoming lily-of-the-valley,
or months before, melting black snow
on the street where you first lived?

Maybe sight has always been a great lake,
too cold, even in summer, to swim in, but look!
You can lean on this rock, a remnant of magma,
stop measuring your life in beauty, and love
the distance turning gold, then orange, then blue.

When I Was Half My Age

I was pregnant. This house didn't exist.
The car I drive wasn't in someone's plans yet.
I barely knew the wind-flared lake at the center
of our lives, the one that quiets enough
to show how weather and death were never crises,
just puzzles to wake out of what I thought.

Now the ones who were then not-yet-imagined
are back to sleep in their childhood beds
on worn mattresses and fresh plans. I'm outside
on an August morning when the sky turns over,
half ringed with cicadas, half edged with the upflow
of a thunderhead about to give us all the relief
that slams clean life at high speed
just before rain slows it all down again.

Wake up, I call to the ones now half my age,
look at the book the wind reads,
one syllable of sky at a time.

August First

> *On the first day of August, I want to wake up by your side*
> *after sleeping with you on the last night in July.*
> ~Carole King

1. In the Middle of the Field

On a hot night, late and blurred
with stars, stale coffee, and wind-blown miles,
we pulled over to the edge of a dirt road,
exhausted from our first big trip together,
the one that would break or seal us.

We walked over a ridge, spread
an old flannel sheet on the ground,
took off our clothes, and let the air
inhale our heat into its own, the stars
spectacular even with our glasses off.
We held hands and fell asleep.

Morning, we were in the center of eyes
large and earnest, a ring of cows
watching us watching them
somewhere in the middle of Kansas,
all of us as surprised as the crickets
flinging themselves across the dewy air
to discover they can fly.

2. On the Continental Divide

The night I learned what graupel is—
ice but not ice, stinging in cold speed—
Vicky and I sat at the tent opening, crying
because this wasn't what we had in mind,
and by this, we meant each other's shortcomings,
high-altitude migraines, the crunch of uncooked ramen,
and a tundra dotted with mean little flowers.

But on August First, we woke to sun, high clouds,
a mockingbird brazenly landing on a pancake,
and the tin cup so hot I had to wrap a sock around it
in the sharp, happy cold at the top of the world
before we packed up and cherry-picked our way down
sliding rocks, startled sand, footholds between
wind-bent trees to find a burrito so enormous
we laughed ourselves back over the divide
and into the gap made of time, refried beans,
the pock-marked table in the back of the restaurant,
and the kind of forgiveness only possible in relief.

3. Swimming in the Oxbow

Four old friends, we paddle our arms on the surface,
kick our legs in the cold underlayer of the water
to warm ourselves. We talk of vertigo and worry
for the child far away or the one who won't leave,
the slow-motion dying of a mother, and all the days
we couldn't fathom shouldering in hospital corridors.

How much has happened, is happening still—
you two coming together after decades of glimpses
in overwrought parking lots after the fireworks,
our marriage long with rough edges between the gatefolds.

The future composes itself from this oxbow's westerly
glimmers, which fall, like stones the currents steal
from the shore, eventually to the bottom
of this lake and all others.

Now it's light on water, a thousand dragonflies suspended
between us and where we parked our cars, where we'll walk
in our wet swimsuits, towels slung over our shoulders,
talking constellations, talking fresh peaches,
talking miles from here to Texas in the last dregs of summer.

Valentine

It's all a matter of seeing what is right here:
your eyes closed, graying lashes on the cheekbone,
then your eyes open: blue washed into green
while the sky turns down its shine, and I ask again,
What are you thinking? Where did it start?

Every question a kind of weight to make
the mystery familiar while the horizon folds back
into orange behind the trees behind you. The delicate
and wild space between us never was space at all,
your words or mine erasing and remaking
what we think is happening, what we believe

time is: not a force rushed through us
but a valentine we can open right now
if we just look at each other.

In Transit

The snowy banks, a negative
of what you might see in daylight,
carve the road ahead from the window seat
of a Greyhound bus, 80 minutes past schedule,
toward a city I don't know, having traded
one airport, one seat, one distorted intercom
voice of bad news for another.

The blackness ahead isn't surprised
by pairs of orange headlights flashing open
childhood cutouts of sloping forests, houses
someone must have once loved, moonlight.

In the parallel life I planned, I am home already,
standing at the kitchen counter, coat still on,
ripping open envelopes to pile them according to
meaning and money, the cat winding around
my legs to trip me into feeding her again.

But here, one landing begets another.
My eyes close, my back relaxes into the seat,
the body so ready to make a home
out of whatever you give it.

How Times Moves

My legs dangle from the bridge
while my grandfather threads the bait,
city lights to our right, Brooklyn to our left.
I bounce my legs in the charcoal dark
and eat coffee cake while grandpa's line
drops years between us and the East River.
Catching something doesn't matter,
he doesn't need to tell me or the laughing waves.

Meanwhile, 1,482 miles and 29.5 years west,
two chickadees land on the winter branch
of a cottonwood, its trunk patterned
an extra dimension by the storm. The birds
shudder off the rain. One flashes her eyes
toward the dangers of food, snow, or love.
I hold my son on my lap, laughing at wild turkeys
between curtains, new before he was born.
The more he laughs, the heavier he is.

Now he drives toward mountains west of here,
19 years later, following a line from instinct
to surprise. A crow lands on a fence post,
in the backyard compost pile,
on the bridge railing in the night rain,
cawing together the beveled air.

We watch, my grandfather, son, and I,
suddenly happy for no particular reason.

Time Names Its Age

When We Were Kestrels

It was easier, of course. Riding the thermals only
required reaching wide enough to make our wings
flush with the flattening slate of wind.

Landing was harder, but you would expect that,
especially in the storms of purple martins, jammed highways
of hail cores, or when the drought broke open the earth
and made husks of the worms.

We persevered, flapped hard to keep aloft, lived on anxiety,
kleed or *killyed* ourselves silly, flooded our beaks with tasty moths,
or the crunch of cicadas stored in that old woodpecker hole.
We creviced ourselves to safety in the secret pile of rocks.
Yes, it's true we couldn't build much on our own, but we were in
fine fettle when it came to making do with others' discards.

We knew the dance of love is measured not in steps but food,
and we were good at it. We knew survival meant
knocking another out of the sky or carrying the small fish
that almost weighted us to death back to a high branch for a mate.
We didn't care if we had to fight.

What did we care about? Leaning into the line of air
that pulled us higher, steadied us momentarily, then ruffled us
into quick flapping to save the day. We were at ease
with the chase, the death, the grasshopper swooped up,
the lilting trill of the call to go north or south.
No thought, all flight.

This was long before we were stilted into humans
who can only watch, suddenly lurch in sleep toward the fog,
trip on a sidewalk for no reason except that old bird yearning
to trust the air and fall.

So Much Could Be Other Than It Is

The bluejay call could be a squeaky swing.
Hummingbirds might just be confused wasps
or the shaking edges of cedars trailing into the woods.
The morning could be ticks and chiggers multiplying
what's left of early September sunlight, and light
could always be what makes itself useful or leaves us.

Lilac could venture out too early, hostas bloom too late.
The drought to come could measure itself in billows
of thunderheads that will collapse without rain
into high winds breaking three locust trees
while the 17-year cicada waits in its shell
for the tip into a communal pulse.

I could be pulled over on a small town's Main Street,
phone in hand, to take pictures of purple streaks of cloud
that only show up as gray fingers above old buildings,
or driving further, to where the road turns back to grass.
I could give up to the bluejays, cedars, sky blinking
with crickets waiting, not waiting, everything telling
its story of wings made to carry light across time.

Copeland Falls

Place a wintered leaf
of your old thoughts
on a flat rock. Wait.

The waterfall takes it in stride,
knows you're just another person
who thinks she knows how to live.

Sit beside the willow, storm-broken,
teetering while water dives
under itself, a green tumble.

Watch what the pine, an arrow
of desire for the sun, does with time,
its roots threaded in eroding moss,

and snowmelt now waterfall inside
waterfall, thunder up close and around,
churning us into the glassy old growth

of water, forest, air, browned coins
of aspen leaves on snow to come,
the relentless ants, your worry
or story: all paper and skin.

Listen: the earth walks by falling.

The Sound of the Big Thompson

Think of it as a heartbeat multiplied
by millions of breaths and stones,
across the green basin that falls always
toward the low, sweet ground
because of gravity, because of light.

Think of it as the night birth calls of the valley's elk,
the pebbles flung on shore, the top of a mountain,
the unremembered in any square inch of earth.

Think of it as the yellow of wallflower, the race
of the squirrel up the tree, the slow lifting of
the deer's eyes to watch the airplane pass, the blue
of the bluebird so blue against the white stone
that it hurts to see and you don't know why.

Think of it as what speed and ice are necessary
to break apart what's ready or not to be broken,
the water made of long-dissolved bones
of what only the 400-year-old Ponderosa saw die,
the clanging sirens of coyotes at that tree's birth,
the sharp diving whistle of a hummingbird dying for love
or the kill, the racing storm that panoramas into
heat caught in a river of autumn starlings.

Think of it as the oldest voice these mountains ever had.

Under the 400-Year-Old Ponderosa Pine

What have your roots
died toward? A desert

of branches, a boulder
for the resting magpie,

a bundle of white flowers
at your base from the light

broken though lost limbs,
generations of pine needles,

all of you a miracle of cells
replicating, bark that expands

in breath, wind extended
all directions, the space

you hold composed
of the first night chill

when you first knew the changing
light itself, a gesture of time

witnessing your passage
over this mountain

The Fire Says

The stump says, *I was once a great dancer.*

The hackberries say, *birds going to Mexico.*

The windows say, *gray stories can light up on occasion.*

The two dandelions in the middle of gravel say, *sun is crafty.*

The metal folding chair says, *I mirror the back of you with pleasure.*

The parked car says, *still rolling.*

The tulips say, *about time.*

The humidity says, *time and patience.*

The wind says, *I'm just an old hobo.*

The thinnest branches say, *chickadees on time.*

The small hole in the ground says, *delight in the dark.*

The old rocking chair says, *time loves us all equally.*

The pebbles say, *feed us.*

The trash bin says, *history is an illusion.*

The fire says, *don't even try to extinguish me.*

The Language of Art

The world reveals itself in leaf fall and story,
unfolds its limbs across canvas or screen,
all we know spoken in the language of art.
How else to see the expanse of dark upon dark
that holds an infinity of stars? How else to feel
the quick lifting of the chest, arms opening wide
in birdsong or falling sleet to trace clouds and light.

Art maps the pulse in the reddening branches,
the misplaced fields of impossible loss and forgiveness,
the rising call of one voice poured into another to break
us open to the song of time's mechanics and mystery
in our bones, the layers of history and stagnation in rock,
the weather or painting unfurling finger lines of fire
across slope or expanse where all roads lead home.

We follow the end of the novel, the nested desires
of ancestors and those not yet born, trying to hear
what is being asked of us over the horizon,
ending one page and opening another.
Then, in the language of flight, we answer.

The People Who Pose in Front of Monet's Water Lilies

A bearded man grins like a fool in love,
his hand on his hip, next to the father holding
his daughter's pink silk cape and pointing the camera.

A couple on their first date laugh at the wrong time.
A guard leans on one leg, flashes a smile
with his raccoon eyes. A small boy halts,
stares into his future. A lanky woman
brings her emptiness to the fullness of the expanse
so lush the man beside her jumps back.

The wild turquoise and pink of the lilies absorb
our reflections while a girl in a polka dot dress
floats past blossoms, hundreds from a single tree,
blurring in the yearning of color to survive.

This sadness holds still in the painted pond,
long changed in its reflections. Each passenger
travels solo in the soft light of everything ready
to darken green, stripping away this season

while outside, beyond this wall of windows,
spring's mottled blues and greens dissolve the future.

Talking to William Stafford Late at Night

Never mind that you're a morning person or 27 years dead,
I hear you over my left shoulder. "Maybe," you say,
then nod. Outside, the pink sky has dissolved to black.
The snow exhales. Temperatures drop. The waning moon climbs
over exhausted cedars. Juncos, chickadees, and occasional
branches of sadness sleep. "Maybe what?" I ask,
keeping my hand moving on the window of the page.

Outside, you see what you always saw: dark on dark,
a glimmer of movement, a low call from where
the air glitters into itself. Behind the curtain of winter, spring.
Inside spring, lilac, hard to imagine. Yet the dirt
still manages to inhale the sky and make itself porous.
We wait together for me to find what I'm looking for.
Not something known and lost but the opposite. My hands
breathe. The steady almost undetectable buzz of everything
sings toward the wide arms of the dark horizon.

World, I could say if I were you, or Friend,
what would you have me do so that the perfect music
could come out, juxtaposing dark and home, song and field,
abandoned house of the heart and noiseless crowd of tall grass?

The Last Light of the Year

In the house, the heat kicks on,
the refrigerator hums a room steady.

The last hedge apple on the tree rolls
down the roof, and the cat jumps on the table.

The friend you love is all ashes now,
waiting for you and others to scatter.

The ideas you have about time or what's right
are lighter than all that ash.

See the budded ends of the cottonwood,
months away from unfurling?

It's like that, and also this: green-black etchings
of cedars waver on the soft sky.

Headlights from the crest of a hill
angle into an empty room.
Here. Take note.

Be still, good heart, bad heart.
Don't be swayed by guessing which.

The Coldest Night

The coldest night puts on her pajamas,
then sits in a worn recliner, weighted down
by the friend who just died, once so warm
and talkative, now a plastic baggie of ashes
on her night table beside the hot tea.

She wants redbud blossoms that are really purple
in an impossible sweet breeze twirling
cotton from cottonwoods in the pink sun.

The coldest night yawns in her chair,
reads the I-Ching and cries at the lines,
"Do you want to improve the world?
I don't think it can be done."

What is there to do but step outside,
where the cold without matches the cold within,
among the stars frozen in their fires
millions of years away while ice climb windows.

In the morning, she will force herself to remember
this is what life does before it opens its heart: it ends.

The Rain Returns

and keeps it promises
until it overflows them.

Gullets run down hills,
layers of rock turning to sand
and slant, swept spider webs

out to the sea of a new puddle
tripped out of bounds until
it's just an inverse dream
of water returned

to the jet stream, curious enough
to fly east for mountains
instead of hills, oceans
instead of dents in
the anticipating ground.

Nothing, no one ever leaves
but that doesn't matter
to the parched or heartbroken,

the aching or abandoned,
the valley thirsty for a return
of what disrupts it,

the body hungering
for the lost limb of who
turned into weather.

Prevernal

The dogs stop. The deer over the loop
of the field pause to note the smell of March.
The absent-minded highway rises west.
A small plane returns over jaunty tree tops.

What do they know about what's coming?
All I can remember are the two turkeys
under the cedars in an ice storm all winter long.

Spring-to-come makes itself a thin sheet
of sadness that melts into all the green.
The wheel of the season breathes us in
before rolling toward its next click.

Sudden crocus, warped and shining,
where a week ago it was just my boots and me
carrying out the compost so our remnants
could freeze like all the old dreams too.

Now the world resumes in birds.

Almost Gone

"Last call," says the sun in its rusting voice,
then leans to the west, sweetening its tune
by forgetting the melody.

The taste of light lingers in the cold.
One crow waits for the shadows
the moon will throw over the brome field
two clicks of time forward.

The stand of cedars wakes with a start.
The dry ground loosens its new breaks
and tilts rocks so snakes can emerge.

The wind moves on, nothing to see here,
while the dark of the dark quiets its old hands.

What's gone seems like it's gone for good,
no matter how often the song returns,
broken light reddening the opposite horizon
like a heartbreak, the song of the bloodstream,
the journey of stone through ocean to prairie,

every flicker of sound and motion always turning
into something, almost gone, almost here.

Time Names Its Age

I'm the broken branch switching
day to night, winter to summer,
leaf fall to rabbit running beyond
the song of the cells making themselves,
the laughter inherent in fire when no one's looking,
the last ember and first sighting of Venus,
the tea cup constellation before there were cups
or anyone to hold their handles.

Purple verbena stays a few weeks
then rushes the door—that's me too:
light on a speck of grass, sun-bleached and
low among the cacti while the impetuous juniper
spreads its long fingers to announce the wind's direction.
Thorns and leaves dissolve to dirt. Rocks migrate
slower than oceans that thought they were home.

I'm elemental, not a set of nesting spoons
to dish out human life, but whatever measures
rain and what you can only see in the dark
once your eyes adjust. Everything in relation
to something: space, magma, tires, ashes under the snow,
sleeping kayak where the packrat family lives.
Snakes underground. Kaleidoscoping weather overhead,
all made of me, old and crafty as a horizon.

Pandemic Time

Pandemic Time

1.

The dog goes out. The cat comes in.
Daffodils so early, and a day later,
sleet clinging to their surprised ruffles.
The ceiling fan spins. Purple redbuds
dissolve the prevernal tangle of green
into anticipation and rain.

I can't remember in my safe bed
what I dreamt or why my girlhood
chest trembles in its 60-year-old skin.

Tomorrow, I will bend low to where
lily-of-the-valley finally matches time,
which is not time as I knew or embellished
but its own flock of red-winged blackbirds
flashing fire over the wetlands

where I arrive again every few days, weary
of my own mind's compost pile, to wander
at least six feet away from children not going
to school, parents not going to work,
and dogs not going to sleep on the couch,
all of us casting our wishes on the power
of water, the possibility of flight.

2.

Around the world, pandemic time
sings at the speed of urgency down
one corridor to the E.R. or in a hut
on the edge of one village,
all weighted in the quiet bones
of those who cannot gather
around the dying, the dead, the grave
that cannot yet be dug

in the place we never expected
for him, for her, for them.

3.

The female cardinal, faded orange,
all alarm, strikes her parade of notes,
each tone dressed alike and looking
for its match somewhere in the field.

A flame the size of a finger tip
on the one candle still burning
at Shabbat service, then,
"Oseh Shalom, Oseh Shalom,
Shalom alechim vachlem yisrael,"
Jack and Susan singing while
we three sing with them,
one square out of 18 on Zoom,
striking the match of our song
somewhere in the forest.

4.

It's 2:13 a.m.
somewhere. Wait,
that's here
or is it? *Who
cooks for you,*
calls the barred owl,
Who cooks for you now?

No one, I speak aloud.
No one at all, answers
the dark blue sheen
and smudged starlight
landing, after thousands
of years, here,
on this window pane.

We Have Prepared For This All Our Lives

without knowing it, like a woman awake at 2 a.m.
who recognizes that the running of the bulls
in her chest is the same terror of her childhood
nightmares where mechanical monsters
tracked her in all her hiding places, then
tilted their heads to ask what she really is
scared of that daylight won't erase.

In her mosaic of sleep, she has learned
to be brave enough to serve shortbread
and tea to her bad dreams to make up for
a mother who didn't or couldn't love them
because something sweet can dissolve the past
into a thousand dandelion parachutes
launching without end.

Her whole life, she has prepared, rehearsed
what she would say to the oncologist coming
toward her with a small box of tissues.
She has steadied herself on the ledge
of a breakup, a pink slip, a child finally
admitting he can't stop hurting himself.

She knows from before she had words
what it is to wake empty as pale clouds
that will not rain or migrate for days.
Also, that preparation means nothing
when the bottom falls out, which was always
falling falling falling away from the floorboards
under the floral chair she found in an alleyway.

But she also sits in that chair on the porch,
listening to woodpeckers to her left, flickers
to her right, drilling their fight songs into trees
while sunlight washes the walls of the world

where she is we, and we are telling ourselves
variations of it's-under-control or it-never-was,
our foreheads bustling words like panorama,
pandemic, pandemonium, even here
in the relatively safe house of preparation
that is not built from knowing what to do
but inhabiting the question mark
of this breath, this bloodstream,
this bird of this time.

Is It Spring? Is It Winter?

The green intrusion backs and forths itself
for weeks, as if it's in question
who will take over the narrative.

It snows in April, and the next night,
a hard freeze kills the possibility
of peaches from the two volunteer trees
that rose from the compost pile.

See? Says the deer walking right up
to the field camera we set in the woods
to show us one large right eye.

Yes, I see, I answer the tiny chip of images
inserted in my computer to bring there to here.
Then I walk out the back door to the tilt-a-whirl
of weather, and once again, as if it has any time
on its hands, ask the sky to help us.

Pandemic Travel

Mask in my right hand, sanitizer in my left,
I venture through the Kwik Shop doors
somewhere in rural Missouri where no one believes
in pandemics, only conspiracies.

Breath to breath, so many scenarios spark danger
and damaged lungs, fear too late at a gas station
gaslighting me or am I gaslighting it?
I strap on my cloth mask with sliver moons
parading across where my lips would be.

In the bathroom awash in antiseptic, one small
ant near the ceiling vanishes into the vanishing
point. I count slowly to eighteen as I wash,
elbow-open the door, and quick-deer it back
to the safe cosmos of the car's front seat.

The raindrops change from long scribbles
to large empty eyes the windshield wipers
can't keep up with, just like me, trying to clear
the weather by angling toward the blank space.

Where have I been traveling all these years,
my hands on the wheel want to know.

Last Night, I Dreamt of Mount Etna

No longer an immense cauldron on the edge of Sicily,
but asleep in a Kansas brome field, and just as big.
My friend Barry and I were studying it on a map,
our pointer fingers tracing the only gravel road
from my house to the volcano 18 miles south.

We didn't know that Etna means "I burn,"
because, as two Jewish people in high summer,
we thought ourselves safe creatures of humidity,
even if our grandparents, our great aunts and uncles,
burned in a Polish nightmare, still sending
shock waves of heat and panic across generations.

We hadn't heard about Morgan le Fay's castle
or other fables and optical illusions as we looked
toward a field risky with the known chiggers, ticks, rattlers
and the unknown in the high pandemic grass to where

the dream mountain waited with its hungry mouth
for something hard to find in the heat of cities
and small towns where we march with strangers or family,
calling out, "Black Lives Matter" across the street
from strangers or family who yell back, "All Lives Matter,"
all of us posting signs along Ozark roads, abandoned
parks, high plains interstates, everything impossible

except the dream where it was reasonable, easy even,
for Barry and I to climb to the top of the volcano,
its fire escaped to everywhere else the world burned.

There we would empty our long-held plastic baggies
of the ashes of our fathers and lost sight, not even
realizing what we were there to make an offering for,
except that it had to do with forgiveness.

The Night John Prine Died

The pink full moon rose over the pandemic
singing through the tree, "Hello in there. Hello."

We listened, all children grown old, but always
looking for something to hold onto, even angels

of the old rivers of our hearts' journeys,
grown wilder in their holiness, forcing new channels

like the holy is prone to do, especially when everything
changes. What is there to do but stand here,

willing peaceful waters to calm us, sometime
in the future, as if that's where paradise lay?

But John Prine knew there's a hole in the world.
We can only glimpse it now while time changes us,

if we're true, into souvenirs of this life,
talismans of something perennial as leaves

beneath the tree of forgiveness the moon climbs.
Come on home, come on home, come on home.

I Don't Know How to Love the Broken Day

I wake to sleep and take my waking slow.
                    ~ Theodore Roethke

I don't how to love the broken day.
Pandemic losses bloom, die, and return.
What I thought was stone begins to sway

like trees that bend until wind has its way
in storms that clean the world before it turns
into what helps me love the broken day.

The blue air shakes and shows me how to stay
while black-eyed susans thirst for light and learn
that everything, like stone, begins to sway.

No wonder when I'm scared, I'm prone to pray
for ground I thought my thinking heart could earn.
I don't how to love the broken day

or storied night that has so much to say
of bats and blossoms, stars and birds airborne
in time, like stone, that slowly learns to sway.

The daylight filters through us, ray by ray.
Like all that blooms and dies while the world burns,
I don't how to love the broken day.
What I thought was stone begins to sway.

This Summer

Everywhere, anger and chokeholds,
burning valleys and double hurricanes,
grief and tear gas leafing out

while temperatures rise enough
to rush body and time to ventilators.

But there's also this: masked nurses
in fluorescent rooms of alarms
saying with their beautiful eyes,

I am here for you,
while the ones they're here for,
answer, as they go under, *I know.*

Your Grief For What You've Lost

Your grief for what you've lost lifts a mirror
up to where you're bravely working.
                              ~ Rumi, translated by Coleman Barks

What did you think would happen
when you let go, or more accurately,
when your grip failed and the weight
of studying your pain slipped beyond
your ruminations, schematics, and chants?

Your grief for what you've lost
lifts a mirror, then drops it,
the broken shards falling slowly
until they turn into small white butterflies
disappearing like notes you never read.

Now is the time to soften your gaze
as you look out the night window
hungry for the light within.

A tree frog clings from the outside,
all of our hummingbird heart valves
opening, closing, into contours of the dark.

The sea of air that holds it all stills
to glass, then whips trees to the ground
and holds them there until the light
pulls them back up, trunks swayed,
but still honorable, each one its own
grief and its own answer to grief.

To My Great-Grandmother Who Died in One Pandemic From Her Great-Granddaughter Alive in Another

1. 1918

What was it like for you that last summer,
the humidity of cicadas endless as the ocean
between the sunny fields of Romania and this
throw-away street in what they call East St. Louis?

Were the clouds too low, the children too loud,
or, even worse, afraid to speak at all
while your husband argued with the other men
at the fence, his flask back in his hand,
lighting counting the minutes from the west?

Did you know it was happening in time
to understand? Did you see a flash of red
while the name of that summer bird escaped you?

Did it even matter that you were pocketed
in a white clapboard box of heat where one little girl,
my grandmother, clutched your forearm?

Was the last thing you heard the chickens
racing across the side yard, chased again
by one of the men or babies while your breath
rattled to the cusp of *Yes,* so far from where
you started, no one left to remind you
that there was never a way to prepare
in a house of gin, weather, and an old dog,
all those cottonwood leaves gone overnight
from the first fall storm that opened up
the seam of the sky, and then—

2. 1988

You could not have known that your little girl,
always worrying about the wrong things,
would run away from her father when she was 16
to the Bronx to work in a button factory.

That she would meet the man who became
my grandfather, Coney Island and all,
that she would argue over pennies and slights
from people who didn't care for her, and he
would go silent or fishing, far away in life
until he could disappear into an early death.
Where would she ever belong?

But she'd return to the Midwest 60 years
after she left to visit me in Kansas
on a day of low-hanging clouds,
seventeen-year-cicadas, and the flash
of Indigo Bunting to climb into a van
with my friends, riding through
constellations of dying towns.

I would make up story for all of us
of a young woman, just arrived in this country,
who married the wrong man, but loved
growing tomatoes and peppers,
sweet corn too, even if the chiggers and ticks
left their curses on her arms and legs.

We would all eat giant burritos at a picnic table
before watching the Paul Winter Consort
sing and digeridoo about the beauty of this earth.

You couldn't know that your daughter's,
my grandmother's, hands flew with the music,
opening and closing, fluttering and dancing,
and for the first time ever that I heard,
she couldn't stop laughing.

3. 2020

If the dead are able to know anything
about what they leave behind, you know
I'm in the Midwest after growing up under
my grandmother's Brooklyn wings.
What are the odds, I want to ask you,
although I imagine you would just lift
your right eyebrow, point to the Osage orange
trees growing those green balls from your time
that, in my time, smash our windshields
in the first weighted storm of fall.

But cars weren't common in your life, were they?
Nor highways, antibiotics, women's shelters,
or other ways for a Romanian woman to save herself.

98 years and 297 miles west of you, in the same
humidity that hatched and was consumed by
a thousand storms, I'm writing from just south
of the Kaw river on its slow and muddied curve
across Missouri, the geography that separated us.

Distances take so many forms: the years
since my grandmother died, the pandemic
that erased you, the pain and heat
that left so little of you behind.

But here I am, waiting for you,
Celia—that was your name—
to tell me everything.

A Year From Now

Will the pandemic spread like a hurricane
scouring the coast, only weakening
once it takes on so much land and life
that it loses its taste for us?

Will the unimagined make itself
as solid and visible as the slats
of this wooden fence, lapis paint peeling,
and none of us painting it clean?

Will there be a cure, a vaccine, a long pause
after we put all the tired and lost children
and old men never sick a day in their lives,
the masked and the maskless, the believers
and deniers, in the ground and in the sturdy
basket of a story we tell of the past?

Will next summer's heat still remind us
of chlorine and watermelon, DEET
that doesn't stop the mosquitoes,
wind that draws in the small flat-headed
black and white bird, squeeching
its readiness to build in the eaves?

Will you still be here, and you, and me too?

What Is a Year?

A year ago, I met friends at La Tropicana
for enchiladas, the first time in two months
the pain in my right eye—a pinpoint of
fire and radiation flooding my temples
and forehead with smoke and ache—
receded enough that I could once again
be a creature of the bright air.

Seventeen years earlier, carrying around
another kind of cancer, I wasn't so much
scared as exhausted and impatient, swimming
laps in slow motion through chlorinated pools
and chemo with its everyday startles and
Hyperdrives at all the wrong hours, and so many
birds slowing down for me or me for them.
I floated on my back late at night, unable to see
the moon or stars because of clouds or poison,
point and counterpoint for the sake of life.

Now my breastless torso and mostly-blind eye listen
with all the others—two phoebes arguing
on the fence, the wind banging branches until
they break, the overwhelming light held,
leaf by leaf, over us—and I want to know,
what is a year? What is a year from now?

Who is At the Door Now?

Just the wind reeding through,
a token of the thunderstorm
in the tree tops, two thirds of the way up
an Arkansas mountain of maples

just starting to drop its first leaves,
August-dead arrows slung into the future,

which is now when I open the door
even if the rain is running sideways,
and the birdsong is hidden and present
at once in time's infinite foliage.

Thunder hurts the horizon, I'm cold and wet
in a collapsed cloud blurring distinctions
between now and later, inside and outside,

but then something red breaks through:
a summer tanager singing fire.

Where is the Answer?

Is it in the speech of the streetlight
so determined to streak its star
even if the fog turns it to glare?

Is it wherever the hummingbird goes
to stillness on a perch in the forest
across the street from the old houses?

Or is it the houses themselves, dense
with overgrowth, leaking surprise lilies
and broken trellises someone once thought
would gingerbread them into charm?

Does it sound like the dense discord of katydids
or is it as hard to hear as first pin oak leaf
dropping? Is it shaped like the curve
straight up this street into another horizon,
no shoulders or lights to save us
if we trip on our way up the mountain?

Can we find it in words like *numerous,
luminous, nimbus* sprung across tops of trees
until deep space swallows up their time?

Is it the space our bodies block
from bird flight but opens louder
to bird song, insect song, leaf song, road song,
entwined in the air we can't see?

Havdalah

What is time to time? At the end
of Shabbat, on our pandemic porch
we Zoom into the Havdalah service,
the prayers opening the door of the new week,
which always starts in the dark

like in that Wisconsin synagogue,
the only light the braided candle
I held carefully, all the strands
merging into a wide flame
as we sang, "Li li li li li li li,"
and cried, because just that morning
in Pittsburgh, people like us
were prayer-ripped from this life

that also tumbles backwards where
I was once a teenage girl up all night
in a New Jersey temple with the others,
telling our Havdalah stories of not being
wanted, our slim arms stretched to grasp
the furthest shoulders on the shore, singing
as we passed the spice box, a wooden bird
with pinholes for cinnamon and cloves,
which smell like time because they're made
of wind, rain, all the old ways we're lost or held,

like right now when I'm huddled outside
with my husband and son, and also inside
this computer screen with all the others
singing across rooms as we extinguish
our Havdalah candles in cups of wine
to make that sound that still surprises us
of fire giving itself up so something
we have no name for can begin again.

There Is a Door

At the end of my suffering,
there was a door.
		~ Louise Gluck

Always. Across the once-green expanse
hilling the horizon, invaded by cedars
leaning into each other in the sun

right before the wind returns
to clear us of all this humidity,
the righteous angst of being human,

which is not to say it was easy:
we were trapped there, like hurricanes stationed
in place against their will to dissolve

into oceans. We were afraid often
of it never ending, pain so fluent
in speaking the language of forever.

We were separate from each other
below the surface of so much sadness
that even the dragonflies avoided us

or we were lost in the timbers of hurt,
piercing our temples or aching in our calves,
keeping us awake no matter how hard we kicked.

It didn't, doesn't, matter if we cried out
or tightened the long vertical muscles in our necks
to hold in our curses or screams,
or if we felt nothing but the bank of fog
become an ocean so deep and tilted away
from the light that we thought we lived here.

Somehow—a miracle, a piece of luck,
a strange happening—there was a door,
and then, on the other side,
we found each other.

Everything That Rises

No One Tells You What to Expect

A downpour as you're running down Massachusetts Street
in sandals that keep falling off in unexpected puddles.
Ice on power lines. The dying who won't die,
then a single bluebird dead in your driveway.
The deadline or lost check spilling the orderly papers.
The part that isn't made anymore for the carburetor,
or the sudden end of chronic sinus infections
while walking a parking lot unable to find the car.

Your best thinking won't be enough to save your daughter
from a bad romance or your friend from leaving the man
she'll regret leaving. Across town, in a quiet gathering
of maples, someone drops to her knees in such sadness
that even the hummingbirds buzz through unnoticed.
The dog gone for days returns wet and hungry,
the phone call reports the CT scan is negative,
and your husband brings you a tiny strawberry,
the first or the last, growing in your backyard.

Life will right itself on the water when the right rocks
come along, so let the bend tilt you toward
what comes next: the bottoms that fall out,
the shoes that drop, the wrong email sent
while a cousin you lost touch with decades ago
calls, his voice as familiar as the smell of pot roast.
All the songs you love will return like an old cat.

Expect to be startled.

Who Dances?

How can we tell the dancer from the dance?
                    ~William Butler Yeats

Don't think it's only thought aimed through limbs,
or core strength igniting the explosion of agility,
bodies honed as swans long-accustomed to flight,
limbs agile as big bluestem. See dance
as lucid as light that permeates everything:

the 82-year-old woman, hands on walker,
who glides, pauses, receives the fresh air,
the black birds pouring diagonally across the street
while she readies herself for the next turn.

Not just black birds, but the street itself grinding
its fresh asphalt against weather and time.
Not just what seems inanimate but the air:
compression of moisture and speed, the physics
of acorn fall, the quirk of the cork unfastening
leaf edge to branch, while the call of the train
threads through the sway of the wind.

The dance always was and is language:
the breaking speed of the crow's wing, the dizzy
of a cold front powering through whatever was
for a moment the safe and the known, the ecstasy
of the universe of water, and how one duck
lands on one pond in the dark. Your thoughts
are simply little snaps of the fingers, small ebbs
of jokes from ancestors who danced in ways you can't
imagine when no one but the goat watched.

There's the lonely man at the end of his life, waltzing
a broom at the train station, the woman in the parking lot
who suddenly puts her cell phone away and skips.
There are new lovers and old ones, tilted broken pairs

and just forgiven-all-over-again ones, making new shapes
in the blankets from their grief and yearning.
There is the clump of dirt falling from the shovel
one woman holds, her sunglasses dancing
with the moving windows of grief as she waits to hear
it all hit the coffin of her beloved.

There is the rush that comes so fast that you lose
your balance and rise in rhythm with "Hey Jude"
blasting from the apartment above
while everyone below sings along.

Dance takes you up in its tired arms,
daring muscles and audacious lungs so that you
can angle life from breath while the first
May peony powers into blossom.

Who dances? asks memory and joy. You do.

Surprise Lilies

Green shoots, pink ribbons
in the alley behind broken mowers.
Flowers past moving-out date,
before school buses slow to turn
into the open slash between the heat
that levels us and the storms
on the next page of the horizon.

When you stand at the end
of the gravel drive, not sure what's wrong,
there they are, never bent or expected.
They thrive on what you've forgotten,
given away or boxed up behind your breath.
They love fences but don't need them
or your attention to petal.

They come on their own terms, a slip
of pink time writing life one quick note
that says, *stop being so predictable.*

Stone, Star, Field

...one moment
your life is a stone
in you, and the next,
a star.
> ~ Rainer Maria Rilke

1.

I thought my story was a small stone, rounded
and black, perfectly fitted to my right palm
slipping it into the pocket of a wool coat

but that was winter, long before we knew
the star had landed, first a spark, then a virus,
likely months ago, likely China, but no matter.

Now I'm a field in high summer, mostly brome
with butterfly milkweed fire-orange.
At night, thousands of lightning bugs
travel and fall green as meteors.

We keep our distance, looking up at nights
when the humidity abates just enough
that we can see the clusters of stars we name

into something we can track: Leo to the west,
a lion that could well be two kites
tangled at their ends,

the big and little bears of big and little dippers
that could be hooks grabbing hold
of what's in our pockets

even if it's just wishes, smooth
as a well-worn black stone,
giving us just enough weight
to remember how we walk on solid earth.

2.

I reached in the pocket of my coat
to find the black stone I took from
an Oregon beach a year earlier
when I sat on the sand remembering Jerry,
who died six years after he photographed
that exact view of ocean and cliff,
the sky half orange, half blue.

Crossing the prairie he loved so long afterward,
I palm the stone, time rounded and compressed,
the big bluestem just starting to soak up the heat
rising horizon over horizon we call days.

Birds sing. Wind stops and starts again.
Stars burn through the tumble of hours
until, dark at last, we see them.

I think my life is a stone, a star, a field
but it's really just a pocket of light we call a body.

3.

We live in light,
photosynthesis turning
seeds to swallows, swallows
to wind, wind to breath
stilling us to almost
indecipherable chirps.

We think we are only stones,
but even rock, far slower
than trees and wishes, migrates.
Weather and water always win,

so come rock on the ocean,
running one way, then another,
pulling us in or pushing us back

to the rising moon, lit, like everything,
by someone else's field of light
bent around the stone of the earth.

What will we be in the next moment?

Thresholds

Charles stumbles from bed to table to bed,
his sister-in-law again explaining to him
why he can't go up the stairs anymore
or down the summer street without clothes,
which doesn't make sense to him since crossing
the threshold of all this pain.

A spray of lightning bugs ignites broken stitches
across the dark while I walk the gravel drive
to my mother-in-law's house to tell her aide
about her bouquet of mini strokes or something else
no one diagnoses because what would it matter now?

When I step over the threshold into Charles's house,
he puts his hand over his heart and bows.
He knows he's dying, and in a week or a month,
he'll be just an outline no one can fill between bed and table,
like my mother-in-law lingering for what will be
years until she also breathes her early morning over.

Outside all of this—inside, too—all the gears of blossom
keep turning, all the doors continually open wide,
and not just to death or disappearance. The world
keeps telling us how much there is to step through.

All Those Birds Flying Off That Tree

When the bottom falls out and there's nothing
holding you up at 3 a.m., you'll need to be strong,
or at least drink strong coffee in full view of angels
basking under street lamps, or poets lifting off trees
like red-winged blackbirds driven by instinct and
the right glint of sunlight. Look toward the comfort
of what light the moon makes between curtain and wall.
Let yourself need someone who knows how to boil water
and sit quietly until enough time pours itself
through you that you can sleep or eat, shake your head
at how this just might be a new cold front sweeping away
the remnants you're finished with, or that common
song that opens the door so wide that you realize
there never was a door to begin with, only enough
of a structure to hold up this view of all the birds,
all the blessings, flying off together to circle three times
—once for what was, once for what you expected,
and a last time for the wonder of flight itself.

The Fight

I yelled. You yelled. You slammed one door.
I slammed another, grabbed my pillow and took
my anger outside to the scared moon, already setting.
I waited there on the porch to meow into the darkness
for the missing cat we were fighting about.

By morning, the fight is an accident, a bout
of bad timing, a crafty animal. The wind rests
its dumb dog paw on my lap, and I forget
my dream of being lost in a city that doesn't exist.

I stand on my cold feet, walk inside
with the cat, finally returned, and go to you
in the kitchen, making coffee. Your face knows
my face, and there is nothing to ask except how
we can stop stealing from our lives.

What Happens in the Dark

You cup my shoulder with your listening palm.
I curve around you, the old impulse to do this,
not just habit or the usual yearning,
but something we need to suspend time
a month after our friend died.

We pump and breathe, lean in and out at once.
The old stars we know hardly visible
through the window, the ones we don't know,
rising or setting, will vanish into daylight.

Later, I will dream of a letter, typed
in pencil from Jerry, not dead a month.
"You didn't fail me," he'll write.
I will try to believe this even as I know
how I closed the eyes of my heart, afraid
of the tree of night he was climbing,
so far beyond where any of us could find him,

especially us in this bed tonight
where we could close our eyes,
but it wouldn't matter
when the heart is so broken,
so ready to be made over in the dark.

All I Have Lost to February

Because the shortest month is always the longest,
February keeps us awake with worries like ice storms,
sure to coat everything until it breaks, making us forget
if we planted all those crocus bulbs along the driveway.

The snow melts too early or late, the bare cottonwoods
shake hard, then still themselves to frame the dark
red fire of the sunset. The first snowdrops surprise.

It gets late later, blurring night and day like evening
fog still not burned off, the light behind and to come
lost to icy curves, days of crockpots and hunger.
It's the month when so many we love die or
were born in the middle of a snowstorm so big
there was no way to shovel a path.

Then, although the ground still smells like winter,
it's March. The view snaps to technicolor,
and all we don't truly need falls away.

After the Winter of No Winter

The parsley rises tentatively, curled fingers
to test the air before billowing too fast
into bitterness even the rabbits won't eat.

The broccoli goes to town, and finding no one there,
except decaying Christmas trees, bolts to full decline.
Carrot tails wave in the wind, decaying underground
because of rain too early, too much.

All March, what should be dead comes alive: redbuds
break out all over town a month early, as if waking late
on a Sunday, then panicking that it's Monday.
Too-green grass, too-cheery daffodils, too-dark-skied
horizons storm through, the planet so far out of whack,
even the air heats its long fingers months ahead,
blurring whether to plant or harvest,
what state, what season, what to do next.

Meanwhile, the dog goes missing, the alarm goes off
at the wrong time, the phone call that matters most
drops and the dreamtime mismatches past longings
with forecasts we couldn't image even 10 years ago.

When morning comes at the right time, the old doves
call for each other in the cedar. We get in our cars,
lean our heads out the windows of speed, listening
for the exact music of the changing air.

Mystery Street

I thought it was a gravel road
lonely as a falling barn with slats
ringing in the wind
while three wild horses wait
for no one to return.

I thought its way would shine
like red glass in sunlight,
so full of darkness it would arrest me
with the clarity of direction.

I didn't want it to be a crowded street
in Calcutta with orange wings and screeching
wheels, a dead end too, while fire burned in a bin,
or for it to be a slope bundled in beige
split levels in a St. Louis suburb.

If it was a street, why not one I knew,
even if I carried such weight on my shoulders
that I missed the red door that was always there?

If it was a mystery what I carried,
why did I know where to step next?

What You Need Is Here

In the last buzz of bees and cicadas, everyone naps,
dogs and humans, snakes in the sunny field,
Osage orange leaves dreaming down.

A bird in the tree is worth more than its weight
in song, while wind sheds another layer of the old
year so that the new one can pour into us.

I wake and start to hum, the afternoon steady
as limestone, also rolling through time.

Old wishes for worth or proof, ashes sparked
upward from a dying fire, dissolve.
The new yearnings have yet to land
in the absence of hunger.

When I try to imagine what to prepare for,
I can only hear the yawn of distant cars on asphalt.
I can only see a spider working something
out of nothing, an airplane miles above
insects stories below, ferrying the past
out of its confines to the next landing.

Something beyond names or wishes sings
to the beauty that passes bird to power line
to horizon, the possibility right now as ever
for love to join the chorus.

Permission

What are you waiting for?
A solar flare to ignite Northern lights over Kansas?
The long-dead grandfather to haul his fishing line back
into the water before the animal of the river turns to day?
Two rabbits to criss-cross the living room window?

Even daylight savings time slows to open its palm,
show you there's no tiny treasure, just a gesture
to mime the streaming treasure of the world.

No one to grant or deny permission. Surrender
worry about the innate character of your children
or imminent decline of your parents.

No wizard to open the doors to the outside
that's really inside, except the wizardry of your own hand.
Nothing to lose but hesitation and meanness to yourself.

Step into failure. Stop waiting for a better deal.
Land hard on your bum, and take your time
getting up again. Behold, from the vantage point
of the floor, galaxies of dust, the steadiness
of the sleeping dog, the joy of the bumblebee,
swept indoors toward the honey
that's been in your pantry all along.

This is Not the Easy Poem to Write

Not like that night decades ago, riding
in her father's convertible up and down hills
in the Ozarks, topless, our breasts happy
in the sweet air that poured through us
thick and variegated, our eyes steady on
the yellow line just to the left, Queen Anne's lace
to the right, the moon hoisting itself up.

Not like the rare ease of waking too early
without exhaustion or rancor, paddling
to the kitchen for hot tea and the sound
of eggs cracking, his hands smiling
as they move from flour-muddied counter
to bowl, even the children up early, rifling through
the pantry for maple syrup or something sweeter.

This isn't easy as my father's last breath,
a slowing train that stops almost imperceptibly
except for the stillness not actually still, then
how the rabbi opened the window wide enough
for my father's soul to take its full size.

This is what happens after the ending, like when
I saw a friend's orange car years after he died,
or the 1 a.m. call from the adult child whose voice
catches on a "but . . .", tumbling in what I can't fix.

The easy poem to live isn't the sidewalk
dotted with rain that sucked itself back up
when we needed it most. Here I am instead,
pacing the deck, unable to sleep, the flashlight
of my thoughts grappling toward some anchor
of assurance in the heat lightning all around.
This is the line I'll write anyway about rain
so hard it amplifies the redness of one bird.

I Will Not Be Afraid of Women

Because I learned early and often that when it comes
to all those falls from *great and gruesome heights,*
there is no one like a sister, and it's worth driving all night,
ten miles above the limit, and with no seatbelt,
to sit at her table and drink her tea while she agrees
that we're here to dance out of the lines, even if it means
we singe our hair in ways we can't remember the next morning.
I will not be afraid to go to her, and to her, and her, and her
my whole life: the ones who hold my stories
like Christmas ornaments, careful not to drop the glass ones
or make fun of the ones made by my children's baby hands long ago.
I will hold her 3 a.m. phone call, when she says,
"it's all broken" or "it's all better," and when I call,
she'll remind me why we're lucky in this life,
sistering me away from *hoarding the horizon* and toward
the new song we'll write, then sing over and over until we're sure
it always existed, just like this friendship, and this one, and this one—
each made of cedar and wind in the long walk at dusk,
lukewarm coffee we drink anyway because it makes us laugh,
or a long nap on her couch in the middle of a December day
when I didn't know where else to go, so I went to her
with my tattered heart and shining breath, to say, "please,
gather me up," and she did. I will never be afraid of the mirror
she is or holds up, and the real life beyond that mirror
where we get in her car and drive for the love of motion.

Everything That Rises

Rise up without fear
to the coffee and daylight
angling over the dark floor.

Rise out of the dream where you are lost
and standing at a broken payphone,
unable to remember the number anyway.

Rise toward the piano you haven't played
for months, and place your hands
on the keys of someone's memory.

Play badly but loud, and let the ringing
rise through your arms.

Rise into the first slant of light
breaking across the living room floor
to coat the sleeping dog.

Open the door into the cold and run
to the passenger door to lean in
to start the car of the day. Stop
what you're doing right now and look
at this raining life rising down,
the air heavy enough to hold you.

Gateway

When the Moon Opened my Life

I was expecting it, even willing it.
I leaned out the second story window
to get a better view through the branches
now that the troublesome leaves had dropped.
I was a child in a city, but I knew, like all animals
with their dewy eyes, what an enchantment was.
The moon exhaled rings of pink light dissolving
into darkness filled with more stars, more moons too.

Maybe it opened my life years earlier,
before I had words to catch what I saw: the moon
watching the sun in slivers, halves, orbs.
I would return to my whole life, once from the middle
of a windy field, walking up a slight incline
to catch up with my friends and the car.

Or from the passenger window of a warming car
where I listened to women singing in another language
on the radio, the contractions already hurting so much.
There was no place to go but this seat
where I waited for my husband to drive me.
The moon would wait with me, or wake me many times,
a flashlight in the dark that made me unzip a sheer tent
and squat barefoot on the gravel, looking up, shivering,
but grateful to be so cold and alive while the rest
of the family slept right through that big, noisy light.

Just last week, I stood on the brink of a narrow beach
and watched the moon turn the pages of the ocean,
wave by wave, far from home, but the moon has a way
of dissolving ideas like "home" or "away." It's just
the moon, the one that returns me each time it opens
the door another inch, lifts the weathered window frame.

What the Mostly Blind Eye Sees

Yes, it can see its way out of a paperbag,
but not more than a wavering center line
on the highway. The good eye has to drive solo.
It sees fast torches where once there were trees
and later, raining streaks of yellow
from the track lighting in the restaurant.

The mostly blind eye isn't bothered by the lack
of definition between sofa and turquoise wall,
the rectangle of green punctuated by branches
filling the frame of the window,
or the absence of a word on the exit sign.
Instead, it sees trembling amoebas
that it swears it saw as a child-eye
falling in love with eddies of dust
singing the sunlight. It sees right through
forced forgiveness or hyacinth exploded
into fragrance and pink too early.

It sees nothing of the future but is smart enough
not to be perturbed by this, or by the presence
of floaters that turn into faces full of better eyes
but not necessarily better views, like now
when it sees the dark green panorama of cricket song
turning into lightning bugs, the smell of cedar
between thumb and forefinger, the heavy drape
of humidity that doesn't lead to rain,
and the tumbling barn sparrow song roosting
in the tree tops, begging the sky for long life.

The Wish

The wish tilts toward the sun, the moon,
goes to midnight concerts of rockers
who sing in a language unheard by anyone
in your town before. It sleeps in late
and finishes off all the pie, loves pancakes
with real maple syrup, and craves non-stop
flights from ice storms on lounge chairs.

The wish flings itself down with more drama
than necessary, a golden aspen leaf in the middle
of the mountain. The wish rains and scatters
like pine needles, rushes away like a squirrel
shouted at for shaking the bird feeder,
then fades into the threadbare pattern
of grapes and peonies on your favorite chair.

The wish obeys no one and barely illuminates
the paper on which it's printed.
It thinks it's hunger, but actually it's the opposite,
sitting quietly on its haunches to watch the sky
do whatever it does next.

In the Middle of Cancer

I thought I wouldn't be myself anymore
just on the edge of all that chemo,
which I walked, step by infusion

for months, scared but mostly
tired, bored, thrashing in the tangle
of small and large irritations. Unable

to sleep at night, I sat up at 2 a.m.,
the sky swirling with tiny particles of light
in the vast field of snow, voles, and rabbits,

later vanished in stray strands of sunlight.
I turned to wait out pain in surprising bones,
the abrupt reverse of drowning

when coming out of anesthesia,
vomiting into the small pan a kind nurse held,
my legs still kicking for no apparent reason

before walking back to the world. The corridor
lined itself with locked forests and waiting rooms
where the sailboat paintings mocked us all

until I could turn my eyes to a mirror,
no longer the one still staring,
but the one being watched.

Teaching the White Fire

The Torah given to Moses was written
with black fire upon white fire.
                    ~The Talmud

I taught my children to name all the things—
a single cedar balancing one male cardinal
on a high branch, calling *this, this, this.*

I taught them "refrigerator," "windshield,"
and "look here, not there" for the doe
and her fawn diving road to ravine.
Listen to the lyrics. Note the mile markers
from Abilene to Limon, and when the sun,
that yellow blur at the end of our drive,
leaves us again.

I told them black fire stories: what's engraved
on pages or below a broken street light
where no one meets anymore to plot escape routes
if they got caught in a dark forest without pebbles
or discovered a metaphoric baby to rescue
from a real river of wailing sirens.

I told them to wear bravery, even if they had to borrow it.

But always we were white-fire creatures,
moving rain to fog, marsh to parking lot,
the sucking mud clinging to our ankles
while we search for our keys with cold fingers.

When my children, now adults, call late at night,
they want to know what I did not, could not teach:
how it hurts to break the old stories, how stale
bread turns back to crumbs and paper reverts
to a single oak leaf dropping on their shoulder

while the invisible visceral warmth of the sun
readies itself to fall off the earth again.

In that caroling darkness where endings,
so mutable, are beyond conjuring, all I can tell them
is let your beautiful eyes adjust to the charcoal
skies of loss, feel what gives off all this fire,
all this warmth, then walk that direction.

The Opposite of Certainty

The Hubble telescope shows us a star dying:
a green butterfly in a tube of black. At the center,
bands of pink burn thousands of years down to one cell.

Everywhere the telescope aims, even in the dark of the dark,
tens of thousands of stars dying or beginning.

On this ground, where is nothing?
Dig deeper: still something, not just billions of cells
but air circulated through millions of beings
dying, being born, carrying on by force of light.

Birth tears right through whatever stories we have for it. Love too.
Earth is made of dying stars, birth canal after birth canal
until death tunnels us elsewhere we have no words for,
just the quick dissolving tail of a meteor, a fingerprint
fading so fast it's hard to say whose it was.
This baby asleep on my chest afterwards,
the imprint that never leaves.

Dead stars turn to lightning, bird song, mud
feeding the hungry river. The dead
are humidity and dirt, discord or harmonics in our voices.

Meanwhile, the living: the face you look at
and think, *Oh, so familiar.* Eyes that have looked into years
of yours, seen the same colors in the retina,
fire in the center, and still are never yours.

All my childhood, I wanted to be certain I was worthy
of being loved, which meant being saved.

Like any great search, you have to begin by hollowing yourself out.
Like any great love, you can't know the contours of the story ahead,
but in the dark you can toe the ground to read pebbles or sand,
a way ahead and, if you're lucky, the ridge before the dropoff.

Neurofibers in the eyes absorb light
while we sit in metal chairs in our backyard
under a gingko tree that inhales this same light.

Suddenly, without knowing why, love, the opposite
of certainty, calls us to our feet and trips us
so we can get close enough to the ground to smell the dirt.

To take air in. To give it back. A natural act, a necessity,
and if we're lucky, a certainty.

All along the way, the scars that weather you, and how beautiful
you are when you get up anyway the next morning,
put on your coat, and go out into the exploding world.

The Sound of Crickets Slowed to Human Time

are a heavenly choir in the key of E,
overlapping a million hands asking, *please,*
and proclaiming, *praised be all, all be praised,*
across this night and those child nights,
awake in the dark, out quick on tiptoes to the
wet lawn on the full length of feet and shiver,
head tilted to the stars, listening to the yawning
plane aimed into the curvature of the earth,
the sweet rotation of the future that dissolves upon arrival.

Crickets sing it all in cricket time and human time,
in falling star time and lightyear time, in each-breath time
and each-space-between-a-thought time. Squeaking hinge
of the universe, they tell of what's beyond the gate:
the last cry of the baby falling asleep, the middle flicker
of the flame in the fireplace we sit across, someone's
good hands now long dead, the conch shell on the mantle
dreaming of the sea, the single blade of grass in a vase
that once belonged to a girl who become a grandmother,
the dust of the windowsill, and behind the panes,
the still-green leaves of a maple on the verge
of its brilliant song of departure.

Gate and gatekeeper, they must be chanting the world
into being when the rain won't stop, the traffic chokes
the journey, and the sojourner forgets how each molecule
is time compressed or expanded to rise and fall
where this false choir of real angels sing.

No Other Way

1.
No other way most of the time, yet the light unscrolling
from the milky horizon conceals what will shine
above, around, below us just hours from now on the longest night.

Snow, ice, and rain refreezes and clings to branches and grasses.
Did you think it would be easy to step outside, to get on
with the day and the weather of a collapsed blizzard?

Not when a beloved watches his life narrow to breath,
the car barely starts, the windshield won't emerge from its ice,
or the ones long gone suddenly are as close as sleet is to rain.

The veil lifted. On the bare branch, an inverse star, one junco.

2.
The river sings through rock and time as we sit at its bank.
Our truest wishes rise from underground tributaries composed
of old ocean, lost beloveds, bravest bones, clearest seeing.

What we know winters over into porous ground.
What we don't know lands on high branches only the deer see.

We turn our faces faithfully toward moonlight and motion,
waiting for what comes next. A junco returns to the harmonics
of cedar and big bluestem. The night and temperature fall.

We remember that this world holds and holds us together
in the widening river of stars, above as below. No other way.

When the Sun Is Closest to the Earth

You live in a room of rising dust that almost swirls,
the same motion you knew as a child
wishing to grow up and see something better.

Walk toward what melts ice, resentment,
that false sense of safety between this moment
and the one that will overtake it
on the count of three.

Go inside and pull open the curtains
for a doe reaching her long neck up to the bird feeder.
Even when fog erases everything into gradations
of gray and steel, you can walk here,
the ground winter-softened to cushion your step.

If you're afraid of time or who it will take from you,
remember how the sun comes close
in the hardest season, bending in the distance
toward blossom, decay, what covers and uncovers us.

Shabbat

Put down the journey of your shoulders.
Pick up the challah, ready to be torn.
Take your place at the table of sunset.

Slip free from clouds. Stop measuring
rain or neon. Lean like the undersides of leaves
into the welcoming sidewalk where you sit,
looking up to the clotheslines criss-crossing
power lines framing the jet trail of someone's story.

In the middle of the night, sit up carefully.
Listen. The wind is a tunnel of music,
the oldest you know. A lullaby of beginnings.

In the clearing of your next dream, behold
a bird you cannot see or hear, perching
in the tree you call your life.

The Midrash of the Heart

I know where to step only by falling
into those green pastures where I'll lie down

like anyone would to rest and watch
the old stories rotate through me,

the ones that act like sky
and not the clouds that cross it.

I'll dream I'm home, waking enough
to catch the brightening moonrise

while wind breathes through the cracks
where this body finally quiets enough

that all the noisy seabirds, aching
to return or roost, can stop their old story
and land on the tips of a new one.

Jericho

How long have you been lost? All your life?
Then you're getting somewhere.
The walls don't fall for anyone who thinks
she knows where she is.

It takes something like music or what I called out
in childbirth, begging life to let life come though.
Or the sound of the new widower releasing a handful
of dirt slowly quickly the long way down to the top
of the wooden casket where a thousand hands
hit the same drum at one moment. Or the breaking
laughter of a two-year-old running for the first time,
about to trip. Or the inhalation of surprise and verve
on the gasp of orgasm in a cold room
where all the blankets have been kicked off.

Knowing the path has always been overrated,
although washing the dishes and counters helps.
Loving and looking for clues are what we have—
the slant of sun across the dusty floor, the stranger
who gives you his parking space in a snowstorm.

When the big wind knocks you down, look wide
for what's ready: the horizon suddenly flashed
by the brilliant wings of an Indigo Bunting
vanishing into the future in a stand of cedar
where you've always lived.

Jericho was never forgotten and never forgets.
Remember how to follow the outline of the city
ready to unmake itself into something better.

Stop trying to hold up all that weight.
Come and sit on this beautiful, cold ground.
Be as lost as the rain making its way,
through the veins of your stories, home.

My Road Worth Walking Down

begins and ends in gravel, volunteer sunflowers
leggy and eager to roost on the edge of car exhaust
while three crows march triumphantly
toward the house in hunger and wonder.

The slopes pool from underground springs,
feeding the dreams I have of a basement
where someone's damp boxes of children's books
dissolve into dried flowers, forgotten immediately
over the threshold of the pillow.

This road roots back to a street in Brooklyn
where the big kids played dodge ball
and the little kids couldn't dodge quickly enough.
It romps up shag-carpeted stairs where I cried out
the new bruises not from the world outside
but from the angry man downstairs.

It surges westward to abandoned farmsteads
of someone else's childhood where the blades
of remnant windmills rust into pie tins
while the present deer and ancient bison keep score.

It returns me home, exhausted and grateful,
where the man I fell in love with so long ago
sleeps beneath sun-faded green curtains
trembling in the wind from the ceiling fan.

My road becomes a path, then just a parting
in the tall grass, easy to miss in storms
that level everything to nothing but a song
of migration and arrival, which is what
the road was made of all along.

You Are Never Alone

You turn your head—
that's what the silence meant: you're not alone.
The whole wide world pours down.
                                    ~ William Stafford

How can you be alone anywhere
the days edge into stippled blues and stars,
the lake carves exuberance into rock or forgets
what sky made it and keeps remaking it?

You are surrounded by the long history of air,
each molecule abuzz with someone's need
or fight for shelter or food beyond the odds,
as well as each claw, wing, foot striving one lift
or step at a time to make home out of nothing.
Turtles hibernate between underground rivers
and six inches of dirt, river-ferried here
for geckos and starlings to cross.

Layer upon layer of the atmosphere
houses stories, charms, breathless ends
or beginnings where you, blown clear
by the wind, turn your head to what falls,
swallows dipping sound into flight,
showing you, *Here here here.*

Gateway

    from the *Tao Te Ching*

1. Darkness Within Darkness

The roof slopes against the dark,
the stars within stars we can never see.
When the world tilts into this,
what can we know anymore?

I dream I'm holding your hand absent-mindedly,
as the sidewalk buckles ahead or behind.
I dream you say my name twice, first annoyed,
then worried. The darkness of our origins wheels over.

When we talk on the phone, I hear the easy sun
of your morning in the melting snow of my afternoon.
Our willingness, always a gateway, but how
will we speak when our bodies lose more
of their easy agility, when our hearts tatter in the wind?

I don't know, my love, but when I cross
the threshold of the plane, the car door, our home,
I will say anything to show you,
*the darkness makes all things possible
and beautiful.*

2. When her work is done, she forgets it/ That is why it lasts forever

What is "forever"?
The shaking of cedar limbs.
The sun skimming the bare branches.
The white fence plank peeling and crooked.
The worn dirt between house and car,
the undetectable motion of seasonal shifts.
Is time a kind of forever work, an angry river
breaking new ground from itself to survive?

I walk from this room to the wide field
shadowed in melting snow and strong snow,
the revealed dirt edging into mossy hope,
the snowdrops clinging to the edge of a building,
the sky's work long forgotten
but its sheen everything to us.

3. *Practice not-doing/ and everything will fall into place.*

The snow is not falling.
The sun is not shining.
The wind isn't. Time
looks at his hand, amazed
how the lines have deepened.
Nothing falls into place or apart.

Shine on, breath, life, rain
so that the air can clear
and the bones can sing.

4. *It is hidden but always present/ I don't know who gave birth to it/ It is older than God*

Where have you gone?
The old friend, vanished
but down the road. The soft mud
hardened under April snow.
In the field, a confused ground squirrel.
In the sky, no big blue heron.

I walk the cobblestone between sleep and work,
the dreaming air sharp and clean with memory.
Stepping in the center of what's next,
the earth that's been here before it was named so,
catches me.

5. Use All Things

Zigzag stone creek, flowing with leaves.
The rust, the faded browns, the grey undersides
come back to this stillness in migration.
The bright blue, saturated in the way of November,
fills everything. Light on stem, stem on sky.

What moves?

Who turns the dial of time from outside time?

"Know the male but keep to the female.
Know the white, but keep to the black."
An acorn drops, then another. The yearning
to live rains down. The packrat rumbles
below the deck. The surprise wind trips
sound, leaf on leaf, the paper of life
loosened and off to wherever it goes.

To use all things means to lose all things,
but also to keep whatever's lost.

6. Hold to the Center

What shines here? The rain
that falls from what's lost?
The sleeping coyote in the den?
The window shade half exhaled?
The awning where ice melts?

I walk into the outside,
my long thought dissolved.
Someone calls out, the hard bud
on the tip of one branch stops.
I don't know where the sun is
that knits all to earth's center.

I only know the way my shoulders drop,
my jaw softens, my eyes close
in the fresh hold of the forgiving sky.

7. The great way is easy/ yet people prefer the side paths.

The side view pretends it's all, distracts
from the banks of the river to the crest
over the horizon. I struggle to see,
and not seeing, forget.

Meanwhile: the neon orange
of the Baltimore Oriole's belly.
The way the cat's white fur stands up in breath
or how young leaves practice their scales.

Who says the side paths aren't the way?

8. You cause it whenever you want

Like sunlight. Like air.
The motion past the window—
what was just here? Hummingbird.
Hedge apple the size of a baseball
growing to the size of a softball.
Too many tomatoes and cicadas.

Don't worry about scarcity.
Whatever small stone you pick up
to hold in your palm lets you feel
the weight and lightness, surface and center
of one body of time.

9. What is rooted is easy to nourish

Let's not beg for rain or turn away
from the drought but lift our hands
to touch the real: the clay of the garden

that barely comes apart, the stones in the wrong place,
the rain that comes with too much force.

Let's plant our feet on the porch planks,
the cement of the sidewalk, the gravel
of a driveway, the stubble among sunflowers
collapsing of their own weight.
Let's walk to remember how rooted the sky is,
and how we are made of sky.

10. Without opening your door/ you can open your heart to the world.

The wind threads its reedy hum
through the space between door and threshold.
I think of my friend's voice right after
she lost her mother. I think of driving too fast
then stopping to be overwhelmed by the stillness.

When I wake on the sleeping porch,
the wind cracks open my dreams:
a shtetl in Poland where my grandmother woke
as a child, sat up beside her sleeping sisters,
and listened to the wind climb the house.
Her heart was open for that moment,
only days before that world collapsed,
and she found herself far away without ever
having opened the door to leave.
We have thousands of stories to tell
of her unhappiness, but what do we know
of the moments that defied her history?
Of the world her heart took in willingly?

The heart isn't a hinge between inside and outside,
who you love and who you don't even know.
Showing you there never was a door to begin with,
the heart becomes the world. Sit up. Wind holds you.

Following the Curve

Poems by
Caryn Mirriam-Goldberg

Following the Curve

Follow the curve of your body
re-assembling itself from standing to sitting.
Your round corners unmake themselves
when you stretch out on the mat, the bed,
the old couch on the porch in the middle
of the night as the stars circle over.

Follow where the night comes from, spilling
dark ink on wet paper, changing your view.
Follow the very horizon even when it curves
into something else, another kind of body
in dappled shadows beneath telephone poles.

Follow the curve of time out of the forest
down the gravel driveway that inhales rain
and exhales daffodils to make more time.

Follow whatever curves life throws at you
as it patterns each generation and landscape
of each body curling to sleep each evening.

Listen to the arc of the tree working its edge
to catch what it can from the sun, and all else
relentlessly curving into what comes next.

Follow the river, taking what we think is fixed
into its mouth and shifting it into what wants to be
unknown again. The river of your life, your body,
aims for land, but is bent on carving new channels.

Getting Started

seems easy as the chickadee perched
on the swing set in the storm

until the first long downward dog,
the arms searching for solace,

the breath too short on the inhale,
staccato on the out breath,

the lungs fluting memory and forecasts,
the heart amplifying the pulse,

until you bend your knees and sink to the ground
like a black colt in the moon grass.

Can you remember the lightness of no effort?
Did it ever happen, will it ever happen again

like birds landing on gutters, like rain the grass drinks,
like the easy sidewalk shadowed by yellow iris,

a world unfolding all directions in the sunlight?

Healing

I'm a newborn giraffe, my slick legs shaking
to standing for the first time.
I'm a raw green snake that lost its skin.
I'm not a happy camper.
I'm a kitten skidding across the floor
to the rushing wall.
I'm fog that can't seem to let itself
burn into iridescence.

Do you see me in a storefront reflection?
Do you think of me when you could get up, but won't?
Do you wonder what "could" even is and how
you can be so new and broken while the world cries
in each crevice to fix it instead?

Listen to the exhausted angel, straining to reach you,
her hand your shoulder, asking the question.
Hear the answering kestrel riding the jet stream,
no effort, all effort to surrender to the sun,
then the moon, each lifting up their reflected
and reflecting faces, then bowing
toward the dirt where everything begins.

Child's Pose (Balasana)

Let your toes fall on each other.
Let your forearms land, happy engines,
parked in the soft grass. Let your forehead
return to the well-trodden floor.
Let your exhalation open enough space
in the underside of your body
that a bluebird could nest there.
Let what comes breathe, tremble, stop,
look around and close its tired eyes,
relieved to not have to be new or old anymore.

Be small, a clam wedging its way into the sand,
while your dark ponytail pours onto the mat,
the air cups your curved spine of stories
in each vertebrae of the changeable future
as well as the dusk you spent on your grandfather's lap
to watch the peach climbing roses in the alley.
Remember the sound of trees flush with wind
as he fluttered his ancient cigarette to the ground
where the birds would investigate death.
Let yourself be cradled in the cave of love.

Sweet child of mine, now, here, stop waiting.
Time is the hand you nestle in. What hurts, hurts
or stops hurting. What you think is real is nothing
compared to the breath of this body, grown or dying,
that holds this child immersed in the sweet waters
of the generous air, the lullaby of attention
carrying you out to sea, and back to shore again.

Am I My Feet?

Am I the running down a long hall of echoes
in an apartment building that holds my childhood?

Am I the grass growing through a shallow river,
icy undertow, sharp pebbles, small stories floating by?

Am I the prints left behind in the sand, or the hungry
gulls floating magnet to magnet above the wetlands?

Am I this river I've lived, the falls and landings,
the inability to remember what happened,
then the life that could have been, and the life that is?

Am I a water-swept upside down tree, the seeds
of the next breath, the open hand of the peony
I bend toward to smell before it's all gone?

Am I simply all this rising, climbing the sky,
then turning back to rain and river?

Downward-Facing Dog (Adho Mukha Svanasana)

I do not like you, downward dog.
I see right through your resting pose status
to how you're just a red-tailed hawk trying
to keep steady in the enveloping storm,
you supposed triangle, you landing base
sorting variegated fears of dying.

Turn my pelvis upside down, and bring whatever
rusting squirrels spring from the center of my body
back to the mama spine. Stop biting the undersides
of my earnest knuckles, the pads of my feet,
my forearms straining toward failure.

You think I can't tell what you're doing with me
between those graceful planks and sullen child poses?
Between the humidity of this moment,
and leaves falling outside the lines of this pose,
these walls and the weather that keeps going
to the downward dogs?

Oh, downward dog, scatter me high and low,
breathing unsteady as winter trying to crash spring.
Wherever you take me, get me back to the
forgiving mat ready to exhale peonies
out of their knotty buds, and then
do it all over again.

I Love This Body That's Not the Way I Thought

like I love lightning, and especially its aftermath:
a horizon balancing blue sky, dying thunderheads,
faint stars, open space—the whole world stretching
its arms two directions at once, just as I do, shaking
myself steady, remembering how this body loves
miles of sidewalk diminishing into a faint path
made by deer with genius for merging the visible.
I love the walk out of what I thought even if
my feet hurt, I'm scared by the blank stare of the sun,
or I've surrendered to how the subway sways its chant
along my spine as it cups this body in its seat.
I love the flash of yearning that turns this body
toward the dark or bright branches of sex or dreams.
All this weather informs these limbs and muscles
in the seasons that come and go, or that came and went:
the mechanisms of cell-building, the three children
from that flint-on-flint spark, the years before
walking sunsets out of housing developments,
and earlier, the fast slim legs that galloped me
down long apartment hallways as the girl
who knew how to tell herself to stay curious,
just as the woman who woke from the old pain,
and put on her walking shoes to head out into billions
of atoms shifting into fire or flower at every turn.

Mountain (Tadasana)

Sway if you must
as long as the legs,
inhaled umbrellas,
stand strong,
pelvis tucked,
shoulders back,
mind a tundra
few climb to the
wind-stripped pines,
child-sized, wizened
for long life, lengthening
toward light like this torso
balancing a pond
in its quiet center,
this heart bursting
into chrysanthemums,
these lungs happy as a dog
following the scent of
the next secret, these eyes,
windows open on
the first day in March,
this breath in sync with
the goose who refound
the flock sailing over
this tree, this mountain,
this woman unsteady,
smiling as the migration
makes ground once more.

In the Middle of the Yoga Studio

Return to your friend, the floor, for a moment
while a plane yawns overhead, reminding you
of being a child wide awake on a bed not yours
in a building no longer standing as you wondered
who was flying above you, and where they were going.

Climb and fall into the animate and the inanimate
downward dog while at your home, right now,
a hedge apple runs furiously down the gravel drive,
and a cat sleeps on the sofa ledge.

Lean back on the bolster, your quads firing,
your scapula angling your back closer together
to show what's broken and shining in the center
of your chest to the world—all walls permeable.

Lift your chest, broaden your collarbones,
legs straight, hamstrings hugging bone,
heart both bowing and lifting as the sun
pulls the tops of trees higher.

In the middle of everything, rest with all the others,
readying to lift from corpse pose while the god
of a million sunflowers turns toward the changing sky.

The Dead Poets' Yoga Class

Don't try to signal Emily Dickinson
when she's in child's pose in the back corner
she knows only as a vacant attic.
She won't see you in the space between
certain capitalized words—long dashes
designating what's beyond lines and breath.

Feel free to unroll your mat next to Whitman,
always chatty beyond expectation or good manners,
climbing his prolific butt into downward facing dog
as he yaps on behalf of all shining beings.

Frost stays at the back of the room, edging his mat away
from everyone. Don't try to make eye contact,
or he'll sigh and rattle on about the need for fences.

Shakespeare goes to the front as if he's the teacher,
blocking our view like the sun, coughing too,
abruptly and repeatedly when he should be om-ing,
and racing his eyes between clock, characters
contemplating handstands, and the long elegant neck
of the teacher, no matter the gender.

T.S. Eliot and e.e. cummings, the odd couple,
pretend they're not comparing their Warrior II poses.
Eliot rolls his eyes when cummings flips into
three cartwheels, eventually crashing into all the bolsters.
He takes a bow to wild applause.

Chaucer hates it when the teacher asks him to model
a pose, each breath a long-winded pilgrimage
to whatever fresh hell or worn-out notions of nirvana
these too-bathed humans keep inventing.

Milton doesn't show up, although Byron meanders in half-way
through the class, kicks up to one headstand,
then collapses into the floor, snoring and smelling
like brandy, mud, and perfume.

The other romantics, particularly Shelley, pretend
they don't know why, although Keats can't help
but burst out laughing about how yoga,
just like love, is an act of negative capability.

Sappho strolls in with H.D., rejects using a mat
and insists on removing her gown because yoga, like life,
should be done naked. H.D. smiles enigmatically.

When it's time for svasana, the dead poets don't stay
in corpse pose, but chirp and crow as they lift
off their mats to roost elsewhere or fly all night,
laughing at us because we don't know how easy it is
once you release the weight of words.

Sun Salutation (Suyra Namaskar)

Rise up breathing. Root your stories
through the smooth stones of your soles.

Let the undertow pull down your spine,
the sea's next wave roll out your breath.

Sail strong, your chest billowing in the wind
as you return home on your own wing power.

Let the top of your head tilt forward as you
inhale in your scapula and exhale your failures.

No need to hold up all these beehives of what
was done and what wasn't. Look toward the horizon

of the windows, then fold back into the other self,
dreaming in curves and blocks of light.

Marvel at your feet before inhaling up your arms
to fly home to the ridge of the hill where you see
trees that could be horses, stones that could be birds.

Let it be beyond naming as you bow,
your palms meeting where the world holds you
all directions so you can salute the panoramic light.

The Yoga of Memory

Let the body elongate each breath and dream.
What's hurting has its own low notes.
Let the heat exhale, the chill encompass.

Let come the picture of a car parked on the shoulder,
orange berries hanging from thorny branches,
telephone wires etched in sunlight, having arrived
from the past to show the future. Even this is a gift,
just like the startle of the cold pond last August
when you were afraid to go further,
but the water called, and so you did.

Or that night in her father's convertible, up and down hills
in the Ozarks, topless in wind that poured thick
and variegated, Queen Anne's Lace to the right,
the yellow line ahead, as you drove into the rising moon.

Dusk filled your body then, as it does now.
Exhale. Evening swoops down outside
of how you make time.

Stand up and walk this miracle home.

Finding the Fire (Tapas)

for Anne

Start with the toes, how they grip the mat,
then lift to balance the sky of your streaming words
dissolving in the fresh air.

Start with nothing but mild exhaustion,
a headache, a warehouse of excuses,
someone else's shawl falling off your shoulders.

Start with a slip of paper from an old fortune cookie
that says, "not what you expected."

Start with whatever small will remains to try again,
knowing you will fail and fall, but welcoming the effort.

Start with wind rushing the windows. Start with
the breath, ragged because it's too hard to hold the pose,
you never could do this, and *this* changes the shape
of your story about a girl getting lost.

Love the art of losing things as well as the hard-won
resistance of your sore legs as you bend your knees
to sit in the middle of the air.

Whatever fire sparks in your body is enough
as the humidity of the room loosens the old skins
of what you could never do, even if you shiver
and almost fall asleep long before svasana.

Start with the beginning of this glimpse.

Warrior II (Virabhadrasana II)

Sometimes only the ragged urge to fall wins
and I forget I'm the granddaughter of a young girl
who sang her way home through the winter woods of Poland,
her voice rough between the tunnel of black trunks.

The forgotten blue heron of my chest longs to rise
from these waters of nothing worth feeding on.
The back edge of a thunderhead surges toward me,
sucking the air out of the room. All the trembling
limbs, stupid-drunk with trying and clock-watching,
stumble to remember their roots.

The other grandmother raced fear across this continent
as she tried to make herself small enough to survive
on the crumbs of what mattered. She carried her secrets
in her pocketbook along with safety pins and stale candy.
Both women died out of their minds, broken warriors who
nevertheless would do any of it again so I could live.

The war is over, the dead long dead, as I tell the buried
grandmothers, the live grandmothers they made
out of their heartwood, the grandmother I will be,
to reach our old arms wide as the canyons of loss,
strong as the occasional breeze that blesses us,
loving as all the beauty we've ever known.

Body of Time

Since the body became an I, it revels in being mine
and not yours. It bends toward drought,
and expands when it rains. It fits itself perfectly
in flannel sheets, around another body, held
in the concentric wind the ceiling fan makes.

This body of time takes another breath,
sends another valentine, ignores another blast
of unoriginal hatred as it learns new tricks:
how to hang upside down in ropes at the yoga studio,
walk across a wet field on tiptoe, or sleep standing up.

It's a month old, or 11 years, or somewhere past 57,
and while it doesn't know all the words to that tune,
it's smart enough to know how it internalizes age
like a tree does as it rings out another year.

It's all the time in the world I have,
so says the swirl of the fingerprint,
the indentation on the left ring finger,
the slight rise of a scar line on the clavicle,
the branches of veins on the back of the wrists,
the heart's muscular clutch and release.

Triangle (Trikonasana)

Wind, come upon me, you traveling vagabond
of rushing light across the pond, rippling calm
as I look up, over my reaching arms, spread
like a great blue heron about to lift from the water.

My face is the sun just over the cusp of trees or summer.
My torso turns up, a wheel of time catching the light.
My bloodstream is a clock of stories orbiting as dreams.
My hands, eager goldfinches or rays of long, sharp light
of the almost set sun. My eyes steady as water.
My feet planted, a good bridge across a river of stones.

Triangle, happy as any being holding the sky and ground
at once before these open windows to say, *here,*
in the expansive angles of breath, and especially
the space in between taking in the world, letting it go.

The Yoga of Injustice, Betrayal, and Anxiety

Here you are, wanting to collapse in the long-term
downward dog of all that's wrong and responsible
for the long wait, the short shrift, and the motorcycle blast
of everyone getting the hell out of here fast.

You also want to rush the door, no memory of how
to trust this body so sewn to disobedience that you collapse
back into its skin of shame, and why not?
It all makes sense given what happened or didn't happen.

You tell yourself this is normal, a faint crack
in the ceiling that slowly spreads while you lie,
corpse pose, of course, encased in a nightmare
that whatever happened is happening again,
amplified in the dark of the dark
until a lightning bug, somehow drawn into
the bedroom of your imagination,
turns on its fire and dissolves your thoughts.

So wake up now in the bed, in the class, on your feet
and let yourself fall because at the very least
the earth will catch you.

Self-Study (Svadhyaya)

Start with the breath that knows nothing but the pulse
of the wind the lungs turn into resistance or song.

Pay attention to what's stuck or sore, gasping for air
or waking up too early in too hot a room,
where the hamstrings say, *let it go*,
while the triceps allow you to reach just enough
toward a branch that will imagine itself into blossom.

Hold a flashlight up in the cave you've made for yourself.
If you can't see the exit, inhale the good, gorgeous dark.
Exhale open your chest to receive further instructions.

Don't ponder the clock, the others on their happy
or sad mats, or the internal weather.
Instead concentrate on the real ground,
what message the windows convey in this tilt
of approaching storm, then the next wave
of change as the damp air sweeps the room
and your tired shoulders, weary of pretending
they hold up some semblance of order.

Go back to the breath, the wind that unpacks and scatters
whatever is wanting, which is everything.

At the end, sit up, lifting your head up last to be
flush with your vision. Bow to the swift cloud
swimming across the window. Study what pulses.

Tree (Vrksasana)

Always a lost limb—the bent leg misplaced
from gravity, or maybe dreaming it's a young
aspen tree in high summer, shining among
the dappled grass broken with Indian paintbrush
and anxious woodpeckers on their way back up.

Meanwhile, the straight leg, a long pole,
a quiet workhorse, holds up the tent of this life.
It sways in the field with the force of all its history
under the new-fallen snow in the metallic blue sky.

Come inside, says the tree of the body,
from where the palms press into the mirror
of each other. *Come here*, says the spine,
balancing its river along banks that shift
with each breeze. Let the forest simply be
where all seeking refuge can return to the wild.

The Yoga of Trees

They do it all the time
because of how they must
metabolize light and wind
into motion and fruit,
whether angled down Main Street,
in Christmas light-festooned shawls,
or patterning an orchard
as the spring peepers sing on.
They've done this all their lives,
from the first acorn to the last bud:
biblical yoga, age-of-Buddha yoga,
died-in-the-name-of yoga,
Mohammed and Moses yoga,
tree-loving and rock-speaking yoga,
throwing the I-Ching with their bodies
and exhaling "Hare Krishna"
to the constellations long before
there were humans to name the sky.
All the trees meeting all the obstacles—
stone walls, volcanoes, chain-link fences,
droughts, another ice age, or traffic jam—
bent on the next twist toward light.
Before we were even seeds of ocean,
they made the roots of the world
out of their green fire
and plowed their deaths into
mushrooms, moss, and miracles,
showing us how to practice
what makes light, what makes water.

Balancing on the Equinox

The golden tree holds her pose for seven breaths,
each one a dazzle of wind, rise, fall, feather, and run.
Behind her, a man on a bicycle lifts his hands off.
A dog tears down the street, leash flying behind him.
One white plastic bag catches on a parking meter,
spills itself to the left, and becomes spirit or sign
before dropping down to trash again.

I stand in the backyard in Tree: my right leg trembling
as it supports me, my left knee bent, leading back
one hip while I concentrate forward the other
to lift the spine. I press my palms together at heart center
and wish for balance even as I start to fall.

The storm to come cups the west side of this life.
The heat of summer cups the right. I exhale.
The golden tree across the way holds very still,
then surrenders everything to the wide arms of the sky.

Half Moon (Ardha Chandrasana)

Two directions at once without going anywhere,
yet I ache toward the horizontal, aspire to the vertical,
each breath a prayer for balance, half moon rising
in the east, half moon setting in the west.

On the horizon of the window frame, the parking garage
holds its horizontal stories of waiting and yearning,
its vertical propensity for release or homecoming.

In the space between here and there, I fall, stand back up.
The ropes hanging from the wall behind me dream
of the warm dirt of southern Mexico that birthed them
toward the softness needed for all the tension here.

The sole of my foot seals itself to the floor
while the tilted torso hungers to align itself
with something as generous as the happy roof of the sky.

Stop here, the moment says. Let whatever aches
for answers set down its many-paged agenda,
pick up its leg to reach toward where the earth ends
and begins. The light leaving. The light returning.

What the Ocean Can Know of a Body

It's known me into existence from the *wide open shore*
of nothing but starlight, and the darkness that forms all,
cell by cell in the shifting container of night,
until I had no choice but to leave for the new ocean:
composed of daylight, yelling, dogs with their cold noses,
the click of light switches changing everything
I didn't yet have words for.

But the air was a false ocean—too susceptible
to weather and time, too easy for a tornado
to push around, or a drought to dissolve.
The actual ocean thinks nothing, says everything
in shiver and wave when I stand at its edge
as a small child, toeing the cold until I fall
in the foam and let the undertow take me,
my *little shoes dangling* from the folding chairs
where Grandpa chain-smoked, until I'm thrown
back into the shore of whatever fear
or miracle is next, this time, and every time
afterwards, ready or not.

I'd return as the body of a child, a woman,
some kind of mammal who remembered
what can't forget it, even if I moved to Kansas,
epicenter of all that's not ocean present, churning
shark's teeth and fossils of ocean past in its yearning
to taste the old and salty humidity of the next storm,
readying itself on any horizons I will climb over
to go 1,000 miles back or forward: arriving on
the Jersey shore at midnight, barefoot, road-weary
trying to avoid broken glass on jagged tiers of low tide,
or entering the bath waters of Florida to float under gulls
swimming the sky, or even jumping into the bracing waters
of Maine to swim as hard as possible toward warmth,
and four singing women in the distance,

all of us aware of *how lucky we are, how precious* too
because the ocean knows change and motion,
distance and speed, and what it is to be a body,
and that body knows us.

Find Your Seat (Utkatanasa)

Sit diagonal. Lean into your heels,
the welcoming mat, the strength
in your thighs now, the strength to come.
Give yourself to this effort while taking
your hands off the controls.

The little war your heart breaks into
in its telescopic pain is just a little war.
Fill your lungs slowly. Wait even when
cigarette smoke climbs the window
and someone laughs in the alleyway.
Reach and remember:
cricket song measures your life.

If you turn your head, a fawn in the high grass:
alone, afraid, happy. Lean forward, sit back
and follow what you know of two birds
way above you, outside on a thin branch
weighted toward the forgiving ground. Listen.

It is not your body dissolved, your senses
inversed away from the illusion of the world.
It is this earth, this room right now,
humans hurt or thrilled, tired and waking,
willing their arms up into the sky that is
your next breath and your last one.

The Yoga of Old Wounds

Your body clings to what waters it first swam through,
no matter how inhospitable: the asana of birth
caving in your chest and forcing you to breathe
in the foreign air that was bound to hurt you.

A slim twisted tree at the center of your spine
trained itself to grow around the stone
(best left unturned) with a genius for dividing
and growing through the metal grates.

What you suspect happened fills in the space
between breath and tissue, hollowing out
your capacity to forgive yourself,
making new contortions out of old dead ends.

In the middle of dinner, waiting for the green light,
or the conversation on the sofa,
each of us is both a single limb and the united forest:
some trees fallen to soften the hard dirt,
some just starting to climb the rungs of the weather.

All our old hurts photosynthesize what we know
to what we don't know until the rain reminds us
there's only a river that loves curves and storms.

Devotion (Ishvara Pranidhara)

Surrender to the sleep that takes this body
down the tracks, a slim wave zigzagged
through milo fields and Osage orange overgrowth,
but who's to say what's inside or outside anymore?

When the motion stops, climb out of the train.
The bare ground leads to a cabin full of bunk beds
with still-damp swimsuits hanging off bed frames.

Then a test you're not prepared for: multiple choice
in dead languages that don't even translate to words.

You go outside, pick up a stick, and try to make
a circle on the bare ground, but it's too dry.
Then you realize you've always been lost.

Sit cross-legged on the curb, your bare shoulders cold,
and try to remember all the Great Lakes:
Erie. Superior. Ottawa. Michigan. One more,
but before you can find out, you're back on board,
your feet dangling out the open door
as the train picks up speed.

Moon spins into view between blurs of trees,
the descent into the cooling valley of night, humming,
Hallelujah to the dark. Hallelujah to the waking
that will land you into one time and place,
where you have one calling always: devotion.

Prayer Twist (Namaskar Parsvakonasana)

Your heart ticks at the center of your mechanics,
its hummingbird wings so quick
even your shoulders tremble
as you join your hands in prayer,

then twist your torso diagonally
toward the first shaft of sunlight after the storm,
your strong legs not afraid to run their engines
in the sweet balmy air of this room of change

where each to each, each without each,
hungers to remember how to turn away
from the narrow ruts of what we wish for

toward the space and length this body knows
as its deepest prayer, before returning
to find the river has, once again, moved.

Let the Body Speak

She still sings the song of shame,
a lullaby composed of knots in the wood,
flesh too large or loose, lamented choices
made in misunderstanding.

But there is new music too,
as she toes the ground of goodness,
tells herself this green light of spring
is her birthright, electric
with synapses and reflexes,
quiet as the shining reach of the heart
that travels beyond her,
then homes in to the center of the chest.

The more she listens, the more she knows
how much more room this music has
to hear the light of one cottonwood tree,
matching its swaying with the sun,
to wing the horizon to better feel
the sweet darkness of homecoming,
to call out to the world: let all who are cold
come in from the hunger.

The Dharma of the Arms

is the upper back, the secret side
of the heart's cradle and lung's steady dreams.

The dharma of the lungs is the atmosphere
that breathes us in, lets us go.

The dharma of the air is the jetstream,
which is the dharma of the hawk,
riding the thermals until sweeping
the wind down to the cedar tree.

The dharma of the cedar is turning light
into shelter for the nest of wrens.

The dharma of light is weather,
whose job it is to turn seed to fruit,
and body to sleep. The dharma of sleep
is to let go and trust the changing ground.

The dharma of the earth is love.

Forearm Plank (Makara Adho Mukha Svanasana)

When I'm hovering above the earth,
suspended on the mercy of the forearms,
the toes propping up the steel of the legs,

when I'm breathing ragged for my weakness,
sure my core will collapse into the soft
grained lake of the floor,

when I'm trying so hard not to try,
my heart slamming against its cage,
blind to where the opening is,

my shoulders take refuge in breath,
my torso makes strength out of not being
strong enough, and my eyes gaze across
the open harbor of the room
to remember I'm not alone,

then I give up, and give up again:
the heat of the moment just some heat
until it's over, and time turns
into a herd of happy antelope,
a gaggle of children pouring in the front door,
a single monarch butterfly, opening, closing,
as it rests on my palm.

Headstand (Sirsasana)

The forearms make a cradle for the top of the head
so that the legs can unfold quickly, bowed branches
suddenly freed to the cusp of wall,
every bird in the torso trembling
in the high wind of its now-exposed nest.

Don't spill me out, the pelvis begs.
Love me enough, cry the horses of the shoulders.
Don't break any eggs, says the mind.

Meanwhile the space between organ and muscle
exhales advice to lengthen like big bluestem,
sways only when necessary, balances the lungs,
now inverted rain sticks, so that the breath
can pour down fear, love, a tree's whole coat of leaves.

Rest here in the lamplight of what you can't do
that you can do. No need to take prisoners.
It is enough, do you hear that?,
to hold strong and calm this length.

What you know now is pure gravity
that remembers underground rivers
with their vanished shores of old dreams.
Wait here for the shy gull to land.

I Sing to My Bones

Half-way through my life,
I sing to this body, these branches
darkening against the brightness
of leaves, this knothole
into time, the heartwood.

Flush with light, translucent
with shadow and electricity,
I used to be a child's limbs and hard sleep,
jack-rabbit fears, then joy twirling me
until I tumbled into sidewalks,

now scars from what I surrendered,
willingly, lovingly, to survive;
indentations from pain that stretched me
into another, then emptied me free.
I've given birth, and not just metaphorically.

My life is made of leaves woven from sun
and water's yearning for itself.
My skin is bewildered by years of criticism,
my size swaying on the front lawn
as the next season opens, and the last one closes,
leaving songlines across my prairies.

When all the leaves fall to husks of time,
the green light still pulses through me:
alive awake alive.

The Yoga of Forgiveness

Stop where you are. Climb down to the floor.
Lie on your belly, the left side of your face
weighted into the carpet, the right side open
to the slight waves stirring dust and light.
The air is free, as much as your lungs can hold
before exchanging this breath for the next.

Ask yourself, "What is forgiveness anyway?"
Someone's notion of no longer building a case?
A platitude you claim to show the world
you're no longer angry or broken?
A doorway out of the room of flying shards
of blame, or humid silences that never bring rain?

Push up on your hands and knees to cat/cow,
and lift your head and tail, stretching your center
into an arch. Exhale and pull back in, reversing
the curve to ask the question another way.

What is forgiveness with an apology, or without one?
What does it mean to put down your tattered shield
and say, *I still love you, I still hate you*
as you push up to downward dog.

Your quiet spine reveals the underside
of the fallen log as you lengthen into
someone bigger, less ruled by snapping resentments
and meek pleas to be let in from the cold.

Walk your feet toward your hands,
holding on to all the ground you can get.
Straighten your legs and just be the odd girl
with her upside-down hair as she swings.
Wait for the moment to slowly rise,
your breath lifting your spine until
you're just a standing human.

Telling your mountain pose to forgive
is not to know anymore while letting out
another inch of the kite, falling
so in love with the sky that you cry
for its pain and your own hard-heartedness.
It's all your limbs inhabiting themselves,
all your muscles holding up the muscle
of your heart, so you can offer up
what you don't even know you have.

Yoga Class Overlooking Four Oxen, Three Cars, Two Pick-Up Trucks, and One Blue Heron

for Gopi

The oxen that sun themselves on the driveway
have prayers for names, love messages in Hindi,
that make them gaze at the tender falling-down grass
with awe and hunger.

Upstairs, mats unfurled, the floor captures the last
slants of afternoon, the light moving its hips
with each new inversion of the clouds.

On my back, my feet dangling high on the wall,
I think of the sandy silk of the ox's coat,
what time it is, and how much my thighs hurt.
I breathe slowly to uncoil the terror in my throat
until we roll up to stand as mountains, still but not still.

Just over our shoulders, the blue heron swims
a current to the wetlands, alone in the grasp of sunset,
crossing one window, then the other
until it vanishes into dusk. The cars and trucks below
dream of rusty companionship and speed.

Then we're lying in corpse pose, opening our hesitant chests
to the dark room, the whole body no longer floating
in our minds and this room, but landed
in the blue light we make time from,
all beings opening the stars of their eyes.

The Yoga of Sex

Start by waking up enough to love the small space
you make together, the bed its own kind of universe
blurring dreams, fear of death, joy of breath.

Reach your toes down, lift your chest,
twist from the waist toward the dark
and thunder sounding its voice to the south,
while one observant cat and errant bolt
of lightning leap down heavy, then disappear.

Unwrap the blankets to feel more skin
on skin, air on air encompassing two
as one. Stop hesitating.

Take into your arms and legs what is ready,
slow as winter lands in the wood,
quick as summer wheels through you,
opening your life to all this falling,
past the way you thought it was.

Then you're just a cardinal, the only fire left,
singing itself to sleep in the dark cedar tree.

The Holy

The holy does not play by our rules.
It bypasses designated creeks, preferring
high altitudes that makes us nauseous.

It waits in the soft-eyed blossoms of dogwood.
It sails the air, mackerel-silvered by a distant sun.
It moves like a diagonally-landing flock
of red-winged blackbirds swooping back up
because of what's written in the sky.

The holy doesn't have arms or roots
we can weed around, although the holy knows
how to hold, and hold on, rock the rocking chair,
jump rock ledge to leaf litter, then vanish.

Never saying, *Behold!* or *Alas!*,
the holy inhabits one long note the women sing
in the small cabin that condenses our voices
into fog clearing before our very eyes.

Corpse Pose (Savasana) at the End of Yoga Class

Lights off, the forest is still. All the old trees
lie on their sides, or stand still, vine entwined.
The wind picks up a scent: blue car, midnight,
open windows up and down hills
in the pulse of travel.

Do you hear how thunder is always on the in breath,
glimpse of great blue heron on the out breath?
Do you know how our arms sing like sunlight
through the hinge of an open door?

The wind picks up, expanding my chest.
Without moving, I let myself land deeper
on the bamboo floor, the cement foundation,
the dirt and rock, the underground rivers
that holds the shadow side of my legs and spine.
The field between shoulders cradles the breath.

On the line my mind threads,
the bird that I call my heart,
finally lands, so grateful to be home,
before rising into the tumble of other birds
and the thunder over the ridge of light.

Contentment (Santosh)

This could be the final surrender that is never final,
like saying goodbye repeatedly to people you love
without actually leaving.

This could be the flat top of the far hill
you climbed to find your lost strength,
or a thunderstorm you watched
from your front porch while the rain swept in
and lightning exhausted itself all directions,
sparking synapses, before going back inside.

This could be the simple blue afternoon
before the stratus clouds turn to ice pellets.

This could be you, a tree crossing horizons,
content as the hummingbird finding the flower.

This could be the tops of the trees blowing so hard
in sunlight that it's clear they've been in love
with motion their whole lives.

Your Body is a Conversation With the World

What are you waiting for? From the first air
in the first room, while a winter radiator breathed
enough warmth for you and your mother,
the world was chatting you up.

You gasped, you cried, you waved your tiny hands
for the ocean you left, and the story laughed itself silly
in each cell until it multiplied into millions more
marching to or denying the heart's measured drum.

Your body watches the moth on the other side
of the screen, drinks the water from the blue glass,
and jumps in its sleep, so much dialogue in this
continuing tender reckoning of bare foot on gravel,
whippoorwill telling the ears of nightfall.

You're always in conversation about how you're not
a separate animal but a talisman of your own place
alongside the freeway and the prairie,
each step another word, each shrug another question
for the lightning bug caught on the ceiling,
the cat leaping from refrigerator to your shoulder,
the wind or its absence evident in the still grasses.
The answers may knock you over or have nothing
to do with the question you're pacing across the day.

Time tells its stories through your body,
so yoked to this love that it cannot stop singing.

Welcome

You come through the gate,
and your life on earth begins:
light wavering green into the hue
of early spring, the growing
heat pouring leaf into form
just as you did, are doing, will do
with scarcity, rain, rivers,
kisses, wind, and horizons
that come each turning of the day.
You stand up in your dream,
lean on the fence, look wide
toward the stars just beginning
to burn through the sky
that carries the world.
A thunderhead powers upward,
spends itself over the past.
You take it all in, welcome
as rain in the tall reach
of the weather holding
this body of earth.

Panorama

This weather will not stop.
You watch the sky and remember
giving birth for the last time,
your view through the window
only of the darkness that leveled stars
and street light, your body like air
trembling in time with your pain.
Nothing could stop the power of life loving life
until the milky daylight set everything right,
burning through fog and time.
A newborn slept in your arms,
and the would-be thunderstorm exhaled
all directions: a dizzy of dark, light,
and the green fire of the world
while you fell back to sleep.

The panorama of a life filled your view
as it does now, as it could at any moment:
the angles of glory, the collapse of clouds,
the grief in rain shadow, the fragment of rainbow
—all exposed like you have always been,
all coming into form like the 18-year-old son,
as well as the newborn he once was.
Across the expanse of a life, wake up
to the silver clouds and greenest fields,
everything held in the arms of space,
which cannot stop.

Respect the Storm of the Storm

Watch like your life depends on it.
The first wave pushes the blackbirds
over the seam of the darkening west.
Uplifting wind multiplies and divides the world.
Flags tatter themselves in its speed. Then sirens.

From the overhang of your porch, wait
for the imprint of lightning to open your eyes.
Surrender to the wide yawning of thunder, the tendrils
trailing the supercell, and the one sweet songbird
at once unaware and aware. Follow
the storm of the storm, not the storm you expect.

When the rotation makes landfall, go inside swiftly.
Rush the stairs to the basement, grabbing the small cat
and photo albums on the way. Call the neighbors
from the crawl space. Press the anxious dog to your chest.
Turn up the weather radio and let the tone of danger
vibrate through your beating heart.

Obey the hunter you once were thousands of years ago.

Goodnight, Texas

Goodnight, Texas, land of expanse and loneliness,
where the sky makes up in height for whatever is missing
in width. Goodnight, tumbleweed and stubborn blue
against the landscape of cloud. Goodnight, billowing light
and speed, the turning away from and toward that spawns
one errant tornado across the home of sage and javelina.
Goodnight, snakes pouring themselves underground,
and glistening vultures, cleared out ahead of the front.
Goodnight, cobalt sky tipping darker as it rises
rain and reflecting pond, where all stories reveal themselves.
Goodnight, old story of old weather, and waking panorama
of what's to come. Goodnight to the whitest clouds,
edged with momentum, and the myriad angles of gray,
surging ahead with danger tucked into their folds.
Goodnight, everything ready to vanish.

Hello, rising stars on the clearest night sky the coyotes ever saw.

What the Sky Is Made Of

The sky is made of soft rain and hard light,
the old yearning to be held, the ancient fear of not
having enough, and the fountain of wind that says,
Something's gone, something else is arriving.

The sky is made of rocks shattered finer than
the smallest atoms of human memory, air we call breath
once we take it in and turn it to motion, anger, or song.

The beating of hummingbird wings compose the sky,
as well as the fluttering of muscle on muscle, the space
in between the rain, the drum of the jackrabbit's heart.

The sky is made of rivers before and after they become rivers.

The Light In Between

Sharpens and softens the horizon
as if it isn't the space between
inhalation and exhalation,
knowing one thing, then forgetting,
or the split second of lightning
antiquing the sky. What we notice
last, if at all. The light in between
holds the house, the tree, the meaning
we make from furrowed field and supercell,
dying father and hospital window,
the threat to come and the yearning
to plant something anyway.
It shows us how to move from lack
and with purpose, gives us the strength
to climb back up from the basement
where we waited for the storm to pass
so we can brew some tea, take in
the carnival glass bowl of the sunset,
saved again, and step outside
to whatever life actually is.

Supercell

for Stephen

Did you think your life was straight as this road,
something that could be time-lapsed into a predictable gait?
Do you try to map lightning, predict when
the thunderhead will pause and fold in on itself?
Have you pointed to a place in the clouds and said, "there"
just before it turned into somewhere else?
It is all nothing, then supercell, multiple strikes through
the clouds while the tips of the grass shimmer.
From the deep blue that narrates your life
comes the pouring upward of white curves and blossoms.
From the dark comes the thunder. Then the violet flash.
From the panorama of what you think you know
comes the collapse of sky, falling on you right now,
whether you're watching the weather or not.
The world dissolves, reforms. What comes surprises,
motion moving all directions simultaneously, like the losses
you carry, talismans strung through your days, singing
of those you've loved deep as the blue framing the storm.
It rains for a moment in the field, in your heart,
then the weather stretches open its hand and says,
Here, this whole sky is for giving.

Finding the Moon

Did you stop now that you found
the moon almost full, floating west
across a small clearing between the clouds?
Did you still yourself in the lawn chair
on the deck and give up, waiting for one desire
to name itself, or another to dissipate?

Where have you been, the beautiful world asks.
Wind furrows your hair. The moon folds under
a cloud the size of a Great Lake. The light leaves
in increments. Lightning bugs thread their stories
through the cedars, which hold all seasons,
whether witnessed or not. The deep charcoal
of the windy night blows through you.

Then the moon rolls slowly back out,
a flashlight looking for you.
Why have you spent yourself ignoring this?

The Bridge

The bridge is made of weather. The bridge is made of time.
Translucent, the color of water, it spans the world in sharp relief
to lushness of green, western edge of blue, rain shadow in between.

Five miles north, the cedars drink up the storm while the sky inhales
old starlight, already dead when it lands, for rock and root,
bowed thunderhead and nightfall, velocity and cricket song.

The bridge is a slim path between dusk and longing, a wide swath
from sleep to starlight, an arm of weather linking here and there,
telling us that reality is always round, circling everything back.

The first lilt of lullaby, and beforehand, the roar of the bloodstream,
the steady clip of your mother's heart above where your own forms,
the tumble and turmoil out, ready or not, to the sharp light of birth.

The bridge arches itself past endings, showing us love is a wheel
that already knows what we learn: nothing is safe in this world
except change, courage, and the willingness to cross over.

What Do You Believe In?

The road, and the tumbleweed that follows it,
the night falling and the stars rising, the last
coherent thought, and especially what comes next.
The brown eyes of the dog when thunder shakes
the room. The wooden stairs from the house
where I grew up leading to the one where I live now,
my mother's laughter on the phone, the sudden falling
in a dream before waking, the dark made by thing
on thing, the chance smile of a stranger in the
grocery aisle, my youngest son's hand in mine
as he leads me down the hall, the threshold that
dissolves when I walk outside, the cranes stenciling
the sky behind the one leaf just breaking from the tree,
all the trees that turn light into something else,
a blue bird quick past the window, a secret pond
to gather at in our dreams, where all is forgiven,
all manner of water, arms wide open,
breast plate leading into the wind,
a lifting of the uncontainable
out of the contained.

Celebrate This Kansas

Celebrate this sky, this land beyond measured
time that tilts the seasonal light. Dream the return
of the stars, the searing rise of summer or fast spread
of thunderheads, the secret-holding cedars and
witness rocks that migrate across the prairies.
We breathe the air of those who spoke languages
forgotten as the glaciers. We walk the fields
that once fed the fish of inland oceans.
We turn our heads away from where the raccoon
hid his family from the storm hundreds
of generations beforehand. This rain was once
a man's last wish, this heat what warmed a weathered
rock enough for a woman to rest on with her baby,
these fossils, love songs of memory and longing
after the beloveds die. This horizon the homeland
of butterfly milkweed oranging in ancient sun.
This creek's trail rerouted by deer and wild turkey.
This wooded curve the one favored by bluebirds
following last summer south. All we see,
the ghost and angel of billions of trails
through grasslands, the remnant of hard rains
where the grandmothers and grandfathers sang
of weather and loss, wars and births.
The bones of this land and the feathers of this sky
know us better than we know ourselves.

What Would Happen If You Walked Here?

What would happen if you opened to something
so totally beyond human that it dissolved your borders
into bluestem? What if it rained and you got wet?
What if you understood not just that the earth tilted,
but that it tilted right through your spine
and that's why you occasionally fall over?

Nothing prepares you for the real.
There's no journey out of this except the one
that separates your bones from your thoughts,
your tendons from the lines of your desire.

In the giant mouth of the dark,
in the opening screen of the dark,
in the bottom of the pot of the dark,
is the dark that isn't so dark.

In the myriad call of meadowlark layered on siren
of coyote upon clanging of wind in cottonwood tree
is also the sound of no sound, too.
Nothing can prepare you for the speed of the universe.
Nothing can steady you enough to absorb even the fact
that light travels millions of years to get to your eyes,
that the dissolved dust of stars are your thoughts
and your thinking, that the sky is so big,
that the dirt is made of bones and breath,
that there's nothing heavier than the sea,
that there's no such thing as exact
replicas in the seasons, and that seasons pour through us
like rain or dust whether we're paying attention or not,
that a rabbit can outrun you in your prime, that language
is only partially made of words, that the earth cannot help
but to keep recycling you into something better.

Dead End

The wind stops here
where land slopes up
to the clamor of clouds.

The animal of the sky paces
in its cage, looking for a way
that will only come with time.

The luster of tree tops already
knows there is no surrender
without risking everything.

What falls away will feed
the roots of what is:
the carefully tended grass,
the wavering afternoon,
the need for answers,
the end of the gravel.

It's the usual way we arrive
anywhere. No umbrella or map.
No way to get found
without getting lost first.

Convergence

The light turns itself over
to the peace of all we cannot see,
while the road exhales dust, inhales
the car over the horizon of wet pavement,
the rain-saturated grass, the rushing
pink light, and the black cows
eager at the barbed wire.

This sky remakes itself in the sweep
of night and change over the next crest,
where another convergence encompasses
storm or calm, dog or car, vulture or thermal
the vulture rides. Dreams wheel over
the sleeping houses. Wind rocks
Osage orange and rooftops.

Ahead, always a vanishing point
where sky and earth disappear each other,
the exact spot of the diving nighthawk,
the motorcycle down the road,
and all else we hear from the back deck.
What are we waiting for?

Seeing In The Dark

> *Barn's burnt down*
> *now*
> *I can see the moon*
>   ~Masahide, 1657-1723

After the fire, what next?
Not the old words, aged with bitterness
or despair. Not habitual regrets and griefs.
Not just a reflection of anyone's ideas.
But what's right here: wind rising
through a tower of cottonwood.
Cicadas motoring their 17-year song.
Golden moon half revealed by
the silver of the passing cloud.

Good things, bad things happen.
News dissolves our vision of the world.
Not to say what's lost doesn't make us ache
or strip our days of reds so vibrant
we forget what we were thinking.

But whatever is lost also brings us to this window
composed of lush darkness, the wind or rain
through the leaves, the sudden chill dissolving
the hot anger or anguish, the pain of the questions
that, left unanswered, might divide us.

The music of the old house outlives the house.
We will make new murals out of the ruins,
mosaics from all that's broken, stone soup
at the center of our next feast.

Nothing in this world vanishes.
Even ghosts, loved enough, turn into angels.
The dark shows us what calls
not at the edge of what we sense,
but from the center of where we live.

Nothing can take away the power of the real.

The Woman Who Watches the Sky

for Joan Foth

The woman who watches the sky knows how light
never slips, but lands with intent, whitening into our view
what the earth says now when cedars rush east, the red
and rock pigments into history. No distinct categories
of the known and unknown, but how they turn together
to bring new birds, a long diagonal of stratus,
and the mountain sharpened by steel blue clouds.
Lower down, poplars send up their yellow call,
shadows of one bend in the earth cover another,
and the road roots back to the slow green of memory.

It could be just west from Chimayo or across the Flint Hills
of Kansas, where the green turns red, the sky collapses.
It could be the weather, always vertical despite how we
move or age. It could even be night on the cusp of change,
the mourning doves emptying themselves of song,
the darkness that clamored for our anxious hearts
dissolving rain into the valley behind the next hill.

She hears the birds. She sees the bands of blue or wine,
the tilting flight of what's beyond our stories, and time's old clock
turning back to ground. When the sky comes, she's ready
for what any given moment of light and change sings
in its rusty voice of who she is, who she's always been.

Where the Road Ends

I've been here before. So have you.
The moment after the big fight, windblown
out of what to say next, while all around us,
the wet green fields mirror the ocean of the sky.

There's only so far you or I can go
before we lose sight of the story we believe,
the past no longer a map for the weary,
the future too far below the cusp of horizon.

This is where the road ends.
There's nothing to do but walk,
the broken-down car left miles behind.
The polished air cups your face
when you look toward the sun,
balancing in the fresh blue of the after-storm.
The wind is a quiet feather, falling through
the space between us. Whatever we feared
is only tumbleweed, so why fear it?

Especially now when I touch the top of your hand,
you turn over your palm to hold mine.
You don't have to know where you're going
to be willing to go.

After the Storm, the Stars

Rise from the Osage orange, wheeling overhead as if nothing
has changed in the fresh heart of the air, cleansed free
of all but wind without end, lashing leaf against leaf.

The rays of remnant clouds burn translucent. Exposed dirt
ages in the wind. The grass tangles a slat from a child's doll cradle.
Paper from two towns away lifts to ferry important words nowhere.

The sky exhales, waits, drops to the disturbed ridge where flowers
rock upside down, the pebbles from elsewhere dream of the old days,
and in the off-and-on cadence of a train's whistle, someone cries.

Tomorrow, not so far from here: search dogs and careful lifting of
sheetrock, broken furniture, bulldozers, power saws, rented U-hauls
to unearth, sort, dry out and save, then clear, whatever's left.

Months ahead to measure what was lost, calculate this day's weather
and read the braille of the stories left behind. The new world not conjured
arrives here anyway, and over this sprawling tree of life, the stars.

You Rise Up To Meet the Falling World

Whatever you lift to the sky, the sky covers:
middle-of-the-night exaggerations dissolve
to slivers of sadness on your pillow,
middle-of-life jolts compress the heavens
into one streak of sleet, thawing into softer ground.
Like the rain cycle that obscures the view,
you can lose your way on old ground or forget
the innate blue light in everything, ready again.
The surface of the tall grass spins in the breeze
it swirls into existence. The present twists down
to meet you each time you catch your foot.
Stars inform daylight or its absence.
We are made to catch the falling world,
just as the earth is shaped perfectly to catch us.

Finding the Question

Is it the wind from the cedars
brushing the wet ground,
the nests of the wrens
tucked into the rock's eave?
Is it the storm over the horizon
willing the dark night
to lighten with change?
Is it the land across the lake
or the rocking of the canoe?
Is it the slim river I dream of, east
of the house where I grew up?
Is it my father's voice just before
he died, saying, *What can you do*?
or the weight of yearning I carried
before I knew I could put it down?
Is it the way I lift my arms over
my head to give up or ask for help?
Is it god or the ceiling fan, nightfall
or the wheeling of stars behind stars
shivering me here tonight?
Is it the love for the earth
I didn't know I was?

Your Road

Walk down your road while darkness
shadows away fields.
Broad sun, at the end of its day,
antiques the horizon.
Each step you take reverberates
on underground riverbeds
that tumble root and death
into dirt and heat. Overhead,
the river of clouds widens,
illuminating the line of your road,
which is never just a way from or to,
but a border, an arrow, a seer,
a container, a hunch, a ballad
about fear, love, and pacing,
and how much you are
what the ground holds: secrets
worn as bleached bones under
the cedars. Your heart storied
as the redbirds that burst like confetti
from the braided branches
of the interior. Take another step,
let your road go far from you,
become what leads and is led at once.
A turning flock of blackbirds,
a shush in the wind, a hand
on your left shoulder telling you
that you are never alone.

All Night at the Truck Stop

Close your eyes, but no use:
the motor of storm
trucks down the highway,
igniting opposing splashes.
Too much coffee all day
dream-blurs spilled neon
and gas pumps, white beacons
of salvation for the weary.
Flashes irregular but relentless.

Far away, over the ridge of weather,
past the moment in its rusty frame
as a lost night with found lightning,
there will only be time-lapsed stories
of a truck stop you drive by,
days scattered over the field of the future,
without remembering.

But now, before the river of decades
streams across the wet pavement,
there is this: *Wait here*, the rain says.
The tumble of thunder.
The pause between the pause,
adjusting your life.

Beginner

Where is that heart,
the center of the field
swung open by the wind,
so we can see what's
still wet and ready to unfurl?

Where's the ledge? Where's the grief
that tears apart all the fencing?
Where's the sudden quiet
when the light through the cedars
dissolves shadows and the grasses
ignite against the changing dirt?
Where's the exact location
where no answers matter?

What does it mean to inhale
this surrender, to exhale into
the sky that holds up
twisting charms of goldfinch
and battered clouds, ready
to change into something else?
How do I bend to get there?

Being Made of Weather

You have no idea what you're capable of.
The rotation born of two opposing forces can
explode down Main Street in any town, any mind.
Fight the front moving through?
Give up and sleep through the storm?
Choices, as if they are choices when it's time
to ask yourself what you're ready to give up
and what you can save: dead photos, living animals,
a tea cup from great-grandmother, a pink-gray
arrowhead found in the rocks along an Ozark lake
in 1983, when someone taught you to skim stones.
Mostly, the hand of the child you lead into the cellar.
Mostly, your own heartbeat, audible as hard breath,
which you must protect and give freely as light or water.
Always, the will to return to the moment the storm
brings you back out to see what you're truly made of,
lift the fallen branch or plank, bend to call out a name,
your whole life waiting for the smallest of motions.

When the Brokenness Vanishes Before Your Eyes

It isn't what they told you, a fracture in the jaw,
or splinter in your finger that can never be removed.
Healing comes whether or not you're watching
in the falling-down house of the body that's upright enough
to live in most days. The old or the new can vanish,
leaving you amazed as you sit on a folding chair,
letting the sun and wind cleanse you.

The girl you are, fire to fire, in the marrow of your bones,
can sit up unfettered on her colt legs, take your hand,
tell you, "Look, it doesn't hurt anymore."
The oldest woman you will be can lean her forearm,
still muscular, on your shoulder, and nod,
her eyes your most beautiful you never saw.

The dead cannot grip weapons anymore,
and the ones still here will lose interest eventually.
It's how the seasons land in each future glimpsed.
The pregnant woman you were can put her feet up,
laugh at the thousands of mosquito worries.
The father or mother, the brother who never said much,
the best teacher or worse friend parallel play.
Scars turns to landscape, bone regenerates itself,
the splinter slips out over time, the lost return home,
and the bad father begs forgiveness. Let yourself
be gathered up, broken to unbroken, in time.

Not Rare But Precious

> *Think of what's not rare but precious.*
> ~Ruth Gendler

The gift of light. Of dark.
The squeaky swing set
that's really a blue jay
searching for love and gravity.
What tells you to lie down.
Why standing back up
each morning is precious
as breath or clouds splintering
into rain dissolving the drought.
The horizontal day that turns
into the vertical night,
the stubble on the path
between the furrows of labor,
hope, and need. Any curve
wheeling toward the horizon,
all the dreams of finding
your house has extra rooms,
the ease of a broken love
suddenly making sense,
the return of a lost locket
from childhood, and in it,
your grandfather's face.
Waking this afternoon to
thunder, the smell of rain.

When the Rain Comes

The clouds roll in,
shadows holding up light,
titled silver at the edges.
Trees everywhere turned,
sidewalks dry and wanting,
grass silvering
in stalks of wind.
The branches heavy
with blackbirds,
the old wall of sky etched
with worn lightning.
The whole fields lifted
to the breaking world
where, for a moment,
all that wants to be said is heard.

Field Love

This love soars through me like italics,
like a chant, like rain into a pond
when I stand in this place:
the red grasses or the black absence
after the fire, the first point of green
from the center of the earth.

In the morning, the deer sail across the window.
In the twilight, the slopes filter dark upon dark.
In the woods, too much undergrowth, too many
fluorescent green brains of Osage orange,
toward the nappy seams of the grass.
Beyond the woods, horizons never skittish,
dream of light tumbled recklessly everywhere.

When the wind pours up and over the top,
the light of day chills slightly. I lean over
the deck railing, over the feathering grass,
for once seeing—like stars surging out
from the blackening sky—the difference between
love, and the defense of love against itself.

Mercy. Daring. Courage.

I have three treasures which I hold and keep.
~Tao Te Ching

I carry my treasures close to my skin.
I walk carefully and fast, pause to catch
the lightning. So much fire compressed
makes the visible even more visible.
To see this is to know mercy, and how
it tumbles shards of glass and stone
to reconfigure this day. To know mercy
is to know daring: every molecule of love
so delicate and damaged, willing as grass
to fly backwards at high speed while lightning
flashes the veins of the heavens. To know
daring is to know courage, how it's equal parts
fear and will, rooted in the dense stillness
of the cottonwood banking the creek,
and the creek itself rounding the horizon
toward whatever comes, trials or treasures,
raining down to wake us up.

Coordinates

I live just south of the poetic,
where the glaciers stopped short, sloped down
to nothing. Now low-flying catfish line
the brown rivers while the valleys go flat
as clavicles edging into erosion and horizon.
The grass, obsessive as always,
runs itself oblivious,
and the cedar trees wave,
one arm, then another,
as if under water.

I live where the sky, dense and
exhausted, complains all smug and blue
that nothing ever happens here,
and leans asleep on its elbows in the corner.
It dreams what we mean: that we can only
locate ourselves in the weather that maps us
but can't be mapped ahead of itself.

Here there's no way to know what's coming,
or what's gone, the big bluestem as tall as it is.
The wind comes. The wind goes. The sun climbs
around the corner and returns at its appointed time.
The windows shake in the storm that can pick up
a field, undress it, place it back down.

When I try to say where I am, I can only
point to the rushing everywhere
the mind tries to be still,
and in that wind, the stillness
that holds a single glance of switchgrass
up to the light before letting it go.

Questions for Home

Did you imagine there was more than this?
More than the grass or the sky?
More than a six-year-old's quick touch of fingertips
on your sleeve? Did you believe it would add up
to a history of torrent and mathematics,
ultimate meanings, causes and effects
intersecting like constellations of the
greatest minds you never knew?

It's just a gravel road in the country.
An edge of grassland washed out of its redness.
It's just a bobcat you missed because you opened the door
a second too late. The breeze inside the breeze,
the dominant gait of weather, the green light in the distance.

Here, don't be afraid. It's not like you lost anything
but the craving for craving, and even that will return.
Where else would you rather be than right here
where the bluebird blurs past the cedars,
and time sheds its old skin so its new one can form?

Chasing Weather

Unpredictable as love that will outlive us,
the clouds fold fast, twist themselves wide.

The supercell spins blades in rusty speed,
then leans to the west, sweetening its tune
by forgetting the melody. The taste of sun lingers.

Crows wait for the shadows the moon will throw.
Wind picks up its luggage, puts it down again
until there is nothing left to move.

What's gone seems gone for good no matter how often
the song returns, broken light reddening the horizon
like a heartbreak or a question we can never get over.

Time chases time. Dirt chases rain. Wind chases everything.
The weather finds us with ease, knowing from long ago
where we live, so why embark on the hunt for what
can never be caught? Let the dark of the dark find you.
Invite the weather in to chase its dreams inside your own.

Entering the Days of Awe

Let us walk unfettered into these days
of sun, wide fields of old grasses
bracketed by sunflowers and pebbles.
Let us step into the lapis sky that fastens itself
to the driveway, the sidewalk, the worn leaves
of dying summer under new leaf fall.

Let us give up the wasteful thinking,
the 2 a.m. anxieties over what cannot be changed,
the waking with a gasp. Let us stand in the morning,
the new chill of the air clearing remnants of time,
fear, reaching too hard or not enough.

Let the wrongs be made right. Let forgiveness
overtake the words we hear and pray, the stories
we've made and tilted. Let us remember this dreaming song
from all our beloveds long gone or just around the bend,
each note engraved with lost lands, singing
of how good it is when we dwell together.

Let the peripheral vision in the days of awe show us
the world, the first seeing of the heart, the last pulse
of those we love who travel with us. Let the wind shake
the trees, the tattered leaves shine, the last butterflies
flash their orange, the first dark blue of night
open into a panorama of past and present light
on its way to us all.

Let the next breath we take inscribe us in the book of life.
Let the next breath you give welcome us home.

Rain

The wall of noise dissolves to rain,
a world held in place by a million falling threads.
In the balance, the fur on the coyote's belly,
worn as leather but marked with a lifetime of fights,
and the lake hungry for new stories to swim with the old.
Lightning angles and wishbones, branches into branches
that mimic what grows or tunnels below.

Scenery unrolls quick-silver—expanses of land
or water, sky and darkness—in the flash that lights up
all the lines of roads and clouds, cedars and shorelines,
before sealing all back together in shifting hues of night.

What seems like the end, again a beginning.
What can't be said, suddenly pouring down everywhere.

Surrender

Give up your house of chance, which was never yours
to begin with, and listen carefully for stillness and sirens.

Release the horses, and crack open the windows.
Gather the cats and dogs, babies and grandmothers.

Go underground and wait. Hear your pulse
and your tender fear as the house rattles.

Hold onto the others, your hand a messenger of assurance,
your eyes in the dark nodding to other eyes in the dark.

When you can't hear or see anymore, breathe.
When you can, climb up carefully.

Open the door to the white god rushing the ground ahead.
Your life glimmering in your chest. Grateful. Grateful. Grateful.

Return

Where have you been, my little one?
Junco on a far branch, tangled in bareness.
A fast parade of raindrops interrupt
the long diatribes of the mind on exactly
how to say it if it needs to be said at all.
The distractions become the main event
all the time the air is performing miracles.

Look: the naked storm has twisted itself into light.
Evening, then nighttime, hangs in the balance
of rows of winter wheat overcoming the horizon.
The wind sweeps clean the bare heart.
Everywhere, the tall reach of the sky returning
us home. No place a placeholder.

Late Night in June

Wind and leaves filter the heat.
A lightning bug stitches a straight line
over the roof. A dog barks, then stops.
Miles and days backwards or forward
south of here, waves hit the rocks of the shore,
tangling feathers and branches in the oil spill.
No one knows how to stop it. Severe weather
to the north spurs tornadoes, and a lifetime's
walk north of that, rivulets of water
finger-slim tunnels in the ice cap, melting
what's on the surface from far below.
The atmosphere clings to whatever it can find,
makes fronts and backs out of whatever comes.
The planet inhales, draws rain down to this
particular spot of young leaves and old wind
as the bolt strobes, cracking us open.

Imagine You Know How to Fly

In fact, you've done it all your life—
the view from above always multi-textured, dense,
promising more than close-ups.

Like this field, mid-summer, watercolor green.
Up close, the deer's contoured belly,
muscles straining against the underside of fur.
See how it breathes?

Now fly forward to the edge of late summer,
just a few fireflies diagonally making their way up
through the white air to blue air, thinning to a wisp.
Drop your arms and stop fighting.

Leave your house behind you.
Go to the wind pouring over and under
the ledge of the sky.
Jump in.

Do You Know Where You're From?

Do you know where the motion
originates in a field of big bluestem,
the single point where the fire began?
Have you looked for your origins
where the interstate belts the hills flat?
Do you count the trucks that read "Navajo,"
billboards promising comfort or salvation,
and cottonwoods crowding a dead river's
old bank? Are you willing to turn
from what's right in front of you
for what only risk and peripheral vision
will show you? Do you look carefully
into the shadowed woods for lost herds
that should be in the field,
and into dying supercells
for the cycles still churning?
Do you watch the light transmitted
from the wings of goldfinch?
Do you ask, each footstep a syllable,
how to walk the right story home?

Blue

Light breaks down everything into time:
leaves into dirt, dirt into stone, stone into river,
river into roots, roots into a single pin oak tree
blown hard in the blue ache of the storm.
Your life changes to air, dust, lapping waves
of cobalt reflecting ongoing night,
silver dimming to gray in the ease of dawn.

A blue circus of joy and gymnastics rushes or slows
the clouds over rocks, interruptions, losses,
makes you stop your car at the end of your drive,
get out quickly, lift the dead bluebird from the gravel
—its inverse weight a sad gift in your hands—
while the blue of the blue takes over everything:
branches baring themselves, stalks of change translated
into grass, and the interior sky called thinking.

The Door of the Grass

for Beth

Where to go now that all roads dissolve?
How to follow deer paths or sudden partings
of big bluestem, little bluestem, switchgrass
into the field so deep that you can no longer see the edges?

No need to answer, says the wind. Just walk.
Just stop in this surprise of clearing
where some other has stopped before you.
Listen to the careful tremble, the heavier rushing
tumbling upward and out from the tops of
rusting rail tracks. Let it sweep back over you.
Your mind only blossom and stubble,
breaking against what you thought you knew
until it too blows free or roots deeper
into something like bedrock turning under us.

Here in the house of the grass,
wind tells the sea in you, the old stars in you too,
welcome home.

In Gratitude

The wind thanks you, unfurling over the worn
horizon so it can billow into night. The stars too,
whether talismans of light dying or just being born,
behind the small birds arriving or staying behind,
who balance gratefully on thin branches of coming winter.
The squirrel in the field, the hidden fox, the mammals
under and overground. The world is composed,
is composing itself anew even in a narrow time:
just before the red-winged blackbird folds
back in silhouette. Whatever act of kindness flies
lands in the heart of a moment, a seasonal marker
to illuminate why we live, a song of gratitude.

Whoever You Are, Come Back

This is what the waters always tell us:
rolling away from and toward us in the dark,
reminding us of everything that formed us
in the darkness before our cells even clustered
enough toward some kind of knowing.
The shine in the sky, on the lake, speaks light to light
in a language of rain, longing, explosions above,
depth below, and horizons beyond too far to comprehend.

This storm lands, face to face, in the center of this lake:
this dream we return to, recognizing the lapis moment
that the stars burn through the thinning clouds.
Whoever is lost is found here. Whatever lines old loves
followed or lost sight of no longer bind us apart.
Let us hear this wind, feel it sweep our faces clean,
surrender to whoever we are and aren't. Let us return.

Light

for Stan

Every act an exchange of light with light,
Stan says as we sit on lawn chairs in the sun.
Gravity catches everything: the falling down,
the fear of harm, the harm anyway along lines
thought tapless, nonexistent, all made from
flecks of light, even our comfortable bones
magnet to magnet to the sun, the moon,
whatever catches the light.

Everything we see travels this way—
the shimmering starling landing on the roof,
the first pin oak leaf detaching, the pebbles
under our feet, the squirrel gathering its winter all fall.
Light makes one live moment out of a dead one
as we sit under the sun, miniaturized from
the eight minutes it takes to land here.

When I fall asleep, when I fall in love,
when I trip in the hall and catch myself
it's all gravity, which loves us all so much
it can't help but to pull us close, show us
the floor, and then how to draw on the light
to push ourselves back up.

Interlude

First, the square of sky opens its wide door
while lightning or headlights ignite the future.

Then the colors band together like animals
of different herds before fading to black.

The distant flash says, something happened,
is happening still at the intersections of dark and light

The shield of sky dissolves, the animals underground
or sheltered in the eaves of trees, tentatively pour back out.

The bats funnel from one set of trees into another.
Life threads itself through time's needle.

In the morning, all light will return, dewy as if
the world is starting over again, which it is.

Climate Is What You Expect, Weather Is What You Get

But that doesn't stop us from yearning
for warmth and long life in the spacious house
of climate, seemingly safe from weather
even if weather built this house. Our bodies
crave solid ground when the actual earth
is fluid as sky, just slower, changing in the dinging
of small hail. Heat evaporates from the sidewalk
on the eastern edge of the cold front, making itself up
as it goes along, just like the space between skyscrapers
invents its own weather. Streets everywhere reflect
the city's hunger and ingenuity in the headlights,
dazzling stars speeding toward us, of all
the weather we make, that makes us.

Flight Plan

My heart trills its plans, a cardinal on a rusting swing set.
It fears how fast the grass grows but knows life also resists
        mowing or fire.

In winter, it bursts red from cedars through snow fog.
In summer, it sounds an alarm in the dense green roar of cicadas.

My heart twists itself in longing to sing its mechanics into
enchantment. It meteors across the sky and lands on a dime.

Perched in the dark, alert day or night, mated or lonely, old or young,
it never leaves the nest of this body, yet travels like weather
        in its trembling imagination.

When it storms, my heart drops into a single streak of lightning
from ocean above to the ocean below.

Two Bodies Always in Motion

A coruscating kaleidoscope of fire, grief,
possibility, and beauty about to be ghosted
in the velvet memory of stars and eyes.

One body bends its light toward land,
the other mirrors its mirage into tall sky.
Yellow-bellied heavens ring jewel tones
of flicker, low notes of boom.

Skirts of electrical impulse rustle
stage curtains across the Great Plains.
What we call a sunbow, neon way of knowing,
thumbprint of the sun, lost ship of florescence
tipping its arctic ridges south
before vanishing north for another decade.

The light never leaves us, only wavers.
No one ever lost completely except
in one slot of time, one way of loving.
Always two bodies: our own, and the world's.

Love Dissolves Your Name

When love comes, the contours
of the shoreline dissolve:
no longer you against the odds,
or your worth pulled in
by the undercurrent
you thought birthed you.
The false bottom drops out.
The lake clears. What lives
filters through walnut leaves,
stills to show the naked light
framing everything. You
inhale your arms overhead,
a gesture of flight and height,
your heart vulnerable but open,
your fingers spread to reach,
the chevron in your back
articulating itself. Overhead,
a flock of red-winged blackbirds,
flashing fire, and behind you,
the silhouetted husks
of sunflowers, long burnt
to silence by the cold.
You exhale through the fog
toward the sun. A blue heron
lands on the other side.
Without missing a beat,
you step into the water.
The cold clarity of morning
restores you, just like love.

Prayer for a New Year

Let the snow, gathered tight to the afternoon sky, relax
its grip and show us the white contours of the new world.
Let the blankets hold the shapes of our sleeping all
the dreams long. Let the cat on the dog's bed move over
enough for the dog. Let the last one to leave the room
close the lights, and the first one to rise make the coffee.
Let the pebbles of sorrow in our pockets grow smooth
in the rapids of our stories. Let the window hold
the pink gold of the just-rising sun and the infinite blue
of the rising night. Let the flowers and stones make
their way to the gravestones of those we love, no matter
how tender the pain of their imprint. Let the quietest
clearing in prairie or woods, party of one or crowd
of crows land us exactly where we are. Let the rain come
hard and wild while we dance in our living rooms.
As well, let come the storm warnings with time enough
to find a basement. Let us remember the heat before
the thunder while the silver light of winter surrounds us.
Let us always notice the blue light of everyday,
reminding us we are not who we think we are but only
and at last canoes on the river of light and cooling water.
Let us paddle hard when the current switches,
and put down the paddle when the moon's face
shines before us, below as above. Let us trust
that we will always be led where we need to go.

Landed

NEW POETRY BY
CARYN MIRRIAM-GOLDBERG

Joy

Cranes pencil the sky. One leaf
tips in its deathcurl enough
to break from the tree.
The trees turn light into something else
under their bark, and small pebbles
rock at the mouth of the pond.

If I see this, do I know joy,
the swooping up toward something,
arms wide open, breast plate leading
into the wind? But what of the charcoal cranes,
the fallen leaf astonished in its twirl,
the dark made by thing on thing?
What of the glamour of a katydid on dead grass?
The black snake with its yellow bottom
under cedars? What about the loud wind?

I lean into the dark of that cool rush upward,
the light leveled on the grass, the sudden meadowlark
song of no surprise, all wonder, the gravity of water.
No distance anymore, only the urge to
stand at that still pond of my own heart
where I've swam for years,
marveling how joy is only a lifting
of the uncontainable out of the contained,
high enough that you can see it.

Winter Solstice: 4:22 p.m.

The blunt air morning-stark,
a glass light that levels everything,
makes me forget my intention for this or that.
My insistent hands home to roost
even if my walk is sodden.
Trees gleam like bronze etchings
rising from the cacophony of
cell phone rings, car tires' turnings.
The night must have its way
even against the snow geese slightly lost
until they find their rut in the wind.

The solstice is a bird with feathers so black
they mirror the buildings, then lift
to land back to this date in time as if time
never left its perch. The motion of breath,
or a wayward finger tapping on the wooden desk
aged by light. The inward turn of stillness,
a slight sway as if standing on a bus, holding
tight to the bar when the wheels mount a sharp corner
and something completely new appears.

Solstice and then the world at this point
flips over, begins arming itself
with light.

The Photographer

for Jerry

Each morning, he goes outside at dawn,
spreads his arms to the sky, asks the day
to do with him what it will.

The single strand he catches and arches
forward in time: a translucent web in the
quick flash of sun on a foggy October morning,

a circle of clouds meeting behind the aching
bluestem, the wind rushing purple coneflower
in the same slant overtaking a whole prairie,

or the light pouring shadow and streak over snow
between the weary lines of trees leading into
the hour of the wetlands.

Each image ignited with what chimes
through his thoughts like quiet fields
a heron rises from, hidden ponds,

the deep night in February as stars
come into focus for whoever is watching.
Even in this field in Kansas, where he stands

alone, reaching out to open the sky.

Borderline

Awake at 2 a.m., pulling off the nightgown,
to turn, wide-angled lens of skin, to you—
everything too much and too little,
the subtle youth of new grass spent dark
around our ankles, the pine cones
yearning for a bed of pine needles,
the crows worn out by their cries.

A firefly staccatos across the night grain
of this room. No hesitations, no place to land,
just the romance of ponds, the silk of water,
and the opening of everything.

Who are you, and how do I cross into your country?

Migration of Animals

After you move far away, you dream
of the Flint Hills after spring fire.
You talk to rocks in your sleep.

When the grasses don't turn red
in October, when no eagles dip
beyond your sight from a bridge,
when the lines of tall trees don't snap
like dried bones in a storm,
you tell yourself that this land
that folds over itself, buckles into
mountains on the horizon,
is familiar, a new kind of home.

Meanwhile, the birds beat out
an oval of air, twist it north
to cover all the roof
and power line of a corner.
You watch, invisible, starting to know
yourself only by your motion.
The earth migrates in space.
Coyotes cross deserts, trees
scatter west, water takes
topsoil into its mouth.

Any animal will lose itself
in too large a range.

Lost

Who can say where I'm going?
My heart opens—a whirl of lift and fall,
a grasshopper flying, the song
that flits sound through the bird
passing over. Music made of air
and pulse, always departing or arriving.

A mourning dove sounds home.
Light on water, a tilting pulse.
Sing sweet, says the still time.
No need to do anything,
says the dimming of the heat.
All birds find home eventually.

The towering of wind layered
like leaves blown upward or down,
feathered like ferns. Do you love me,
have you always? Dreaming like
the lone red trunk in the forest
of antiqued black, dreaming like the surface
of water, right before the blue heron slams
toward dinner, dreaming like my hand
on my father's knee to feel his pulse
right before he died. Will you be true to me?
Do I know how to be true to you?

The answer: bird song on the diagonal
into the future, which is always slanted
like someone dreaming over the next bend.

The answer: the tree of life, not over the ridge
or outside of my own spine. Leaning into
the soft breeze, steeled against the heat,
ready to ignite into fruit and fire.

Lullaby for the Changing Moon

Sometimes you hide your back,
and just show elbows and knees,
one shining side of your face until
just the closed eye is left.
Then you disappear altogether

until you return.
The outer edge of your arm, then
half of you wet in the torn gauze of cloud.
A pebble of light tossed into the sky,
iridescent like the color of lips
juxtaposed with infinity.

Somewhere a pond thaws.
You have been sleeping
in the tree slung overhead until
invisible hands herd the clouds
past the window of your face.

In daylight, white on white,
no separation.

My Daughter Six Years Before Her Birth

At age 20, her eyes
wet, says, "Mom,
I don't know what
I'm doing with my life."

I reach out to touch
her head, all those
black curls coiled
in the sunlight.

Six years before her birth
I see in the dark
her face asleep
in her father's.

I know already how
she'll lie awake in my arms
as I walk back
and forth the night
in the kitchen,

or run to me, her body
all gazelle, her heart
all ocean, with handfuls
of seashells she's discovered,
a dead ocean contained in each.

Sixteen years after her birth
I watch her twirl in three-inch heels
and a sapphire dress, time
shining out her eyes.

"Yes," I tell her again,
always, especially as the undertow
pulls time back and reveals
the space we call love.

What Isn't a Prayer Anymore?

I hold the speckled gray stone in my palm,
everything smooth and rough at once—
the wind always some kind of shawl, and what lifts
the shawl, throws it off the body. The things that make
you tremble, the things that tell you god is just
a form of shivering or suddenly being warmed
from a distant fire near the small pond
in the forest of your heart.

I stand on the back deck in zero degrees
in my thick blue slippers, the empty compost bowl
in my right hand, the door knob in my left,
the dog inside so concerned, and the cat
only fixated on the panoramic intensity
she sees across the bird feeder,
all between sun and wind, the inside
and outside. What isn't a prayer anymore?

The way of sitting cross-legged in the chair
at the meeting, or the stoplight red under ice
as if that red is alive. The short grass,
the long grass, held in the icy tips of light.
The candle burning on the table, the old
painting done by my mother-in-law before
she gave birth to my husband, the child
carrying the CD he'll listen to repeatedly
for one Irish ballad.

After Woody Went Back to the Forest

for Woody

Ponderosa pine made of wind, loss,
quick brightnesses that illuminate
what no one sees but the pine needles
that make a bed for no one in particular,
so why not you? Is that where you are,
the slope of the sky filled with magpie song?
Or do you wait in the sweeping blue silk
of the river so far behind?

Is your memory shimmering like our idea
of love, taking into its mouth new land,
right in the confluence between mind and the grainy turn
of the seasons? Are you ample with the light and heat
you knew from fighting fire at high altitudes?

Or are you beyond metaphor, having turned into
the air itself spanning these hundreds of miles
between the weighted humidity of Midwestern rivers
and the clear echoes of the Rockies?

Are you landing all the time, are you rising
back up again, are you coming into mind
or going back out, no longer solid as flesh
but more like time itself, on the hoof,
unable to wait for the ending
to our old stories about you?

Just-Doing-That-Moon

The cupboards licked clean by grief,
I open the front door anyway.
Ice wind, hot sun—too much or too little.
I close the door.

Give me an hour, and the cupboards
fill again with cans and boxes ready
to warm the belly, add weight
to the thin blue glass dinner plates
while the wind turns balmy,
the sky seamlessly white,
both of which scour the ground
which wants something planted
but not just yet.

Close my eyes, the dreams bleed
and quicken, just like this March weather:
a rush overhead as if the bare sycamore
is a canopy of faces, all the ancestors
at their tea party. Open my eyes,
and I can't remember anything
but this old dog grief, chasing rabbits
in his sleep, always hungry.

When I open the night door to the
Just-doing-that moon, I forget all but
the surprise of snow at midnight
that falls so lightly, it can rest on
the lip of the first daffodil.

What Isn't Possible?

Not the wind, as possible as breath, as the earth
rotating on its axis, or the kiss right after
the kiss before. As possible as the dark,
which is as possible as the light.
As possible as bird song, clouds unraveling
or the dog chasing the rabbit across
the wet glistening we call a lawn in early morning.
The chase as possible as it is predictable,
and the predictable as possible as
reliable, trustworthy, usual.

The unusual as possible as wind which tatters
a red flag posted high in a well-to-do older neighborhood
where college boys ride mowers down the sidewalk solemnly
past winos from the universe next door that comes
from a seed of different, not fewer, possibilities.

What's scarred over? Everything.
What's possible to heal beyond a trace? Nothing.
But all around the skin, the land,
the bodies in motion, even the seamless wind itself
moving from its deep wounds and the ever-present possibility
into sometime etched with history
in its old dog hunger.

Advice for the Material World

Don't be afraid to be beautiful,
I tell the wind chimes.

Feel free to relax,
I tell the table.

Go to the forest
and find a clearing,
I tell the rug.

To one glass pane, I say,
lean back and let the silver sun
tell you its stories.

The same for the river banks, the rocks
set apart in the grass, the curvature
of bones in wings.

Water, I say, stop rushing away
from memory; it's your nature.

The crest of the horizon, visit
on time even if time shifts shadows
on buildings.

Shadows and buildings,
remember, you're no different
from the trees and sidewalks
you look down on.

Lines between the cobblestones,
don't ever forget you're just as important
if not more so than the fleshy brick.

What I cannot see beneath or behind, be safe,
and tilt open your brown eyes in the dark night.
We're watching for you, many of us, and wishing you well.

Nouns I Have Loved

Helicopter at night. Lion cub. Straw blanketing
the grass. Wind. A building made of ice. Sirens.
The stir of a wooden spoon. Eyebrows in
the sunlight. Shoelaces. Down in any form.
Drapes like spilled water. The ball of the foot.
Messages on the sides of pens. Charcoal briquettes.
Bells that sound like peacocks. A basketball skimming
through the rim. Brown lips. Terrycloth.
The slope of velvet lawns. Any rooftop. Lounge chairs
shaped like lizards. Incense and icicles. Balconies,
especially aloof ones. Round windows. Rain at night.
Fingertips of newborns. Wool socks. Marbled
green paper boxes with lids. Whipped cream melting
in hot chocolate. Shoulder blades. Wood just cut.
T-shirts with messages written in other languages.
Turquoise. Kisses. Hummingbird wings. Any tapestry.
The arch of a spine. Pink flamingos. Light sockets
in all the right places. Laundry detergent.
Snow melting in the street under a bicycle tire.
A slim valley holding the snow of weeks ago.
One last hyacinth on the north ledge, unaware
of what time it is.

The Life You Could Be Living
(If You Weren't Living This One)

The life you could be living aches in its compression,
tires of being a spark, an asteroid,
a falling raindrop bouncing when it hits.
It's wound tight between muscle and sinew,
lodged in the happy gaps of a synapse.
It's fluid like flowers. It sounds like geese
out of sight. It's marvelous as falling asleep
when exhausted, and it foreshadows your dreams
like a stray piece of sunlight or an unnoticed icicle.

Pull apart the paper vignettes and subtle
understandings. Find a favorite shoe lost
decades ago, a line to an old song,
and behind that, the melody that once
made you lift your arms and twirl
in your childhood bedroom after dark.

This life startles you with its foreign tongue
of traumas and kisses, its vulnerable eyes
staring into yours for mercy as it lies down beside you,
tries to say—although it doesn't know your language—
that it's okay how it turned out, that it's still here,
and despite its wish to be lived,
it's not going anywhere.

Billboards

Billboards on roads no one drives anymore,
caving into neglect, the letters faded as old irises,
the cracking wooden edges framing
what once saved lives, flashed secrets
of how to live right in this world.

Business cards out of control:
a kettle of fish, a whole lobster, a box of chocolates,
a chest of antique lace, a warning against
pregnancy or drugs, arthritis, the anger of the Lord,
a good night's sleep for once, thrown rolls
342 miles east, condos for sale, winning basketball teams,
stores to shop like you mean it, the Mario Lanza museum,
sleepwear, tires, abortion kills, and the oldest
continuously running train in America.

What would you say to the rushing sea of drivers
flashing through your life at the speed of desire and fear?
Would you display beloved books, searches for
a lost locket your grandmother gave you
when you were five and broke your arm,
the best discovery of your life, and how it turned out
to be ordinary, like watching your father take his last breath?
Would you list your beloveds as talismans to keep them safe?
Would you ask forgiveness, directions, a gathering of forces
or simply for an empty billboard to grant you
a place to live while life weathered you?

The Dreaming Land

I dream of spring, when the sky dampens
the seeds of gathering heat, the diving crow
aims toward what was just born, and
even the driveway gravel glitters in the stark
white light between storm and night.
I dream of the winter's black-and-white landscape
scribbled green, punctured by the maroon tip of root
in a field cleaned black with fire while
the cottonwoods unfurl their pale green hearts.

This land dreams sky, a shifting infusion
of shadow on cloud, despite the unreliability
of rain or clarity. The deer dream fawns.
The fawns dream flight as they walk the through-line
of the horizon. The horizon never stops dreaming,
its sleep a progression of filtering color through space.

The dream always dreams possibility
juxtaposed against decay, lightning, first
redbud blossom or starling feather stuck on a rooftop.
The rooftop dreams, belly up, to the sky,
its dream a song of shelter and risk.

The sky dreams light rolling away from dark,
dark rolling away from light, expansive as sorrow
that permeates the porous souls of everything
from weather to the dog left alone in the living room
while I step outside into the dizzy of bird call,
flocks pouring down onto branches
swollen with the hard dreams of blossom.

Self-Portrait as River of Starlings

No right angles. All curve over the dead
spaces, the fast moving gaps, the halting ones.
Not one but many pouring down like manna
from the surprised clouds, like water, like inverse stars
suddenly roosting in all the strategic places
at the last minute. Bees broken from the hive
or wind lost. Sadness that can't ever get
its wings pointed in the right direction to depart.
Tunnels of us spinning through archways of us,
sharp against the January blue, straining like
a mind made to collect itself, find the origin of
this river fingering back to the eastern horizon
without being blinded by its own addictive beauty
magnetically tracing the river below, the whole world
a spoil of predators and wetlands, sunlight sleek like
sex finding its rhythm, all of us ribboning
toward the dying heat in the dirt.

Self-Portrait Before Birth

The roundness of this pond carrying its own landscape
of sound: mountains in wind, old vacant lots,
roads under construction, roots growing through each other.
All the trees shedding cells to cling to the new one
until they aren't themselves anymore. Toes tumble overhead.
A resting place, hot and round; a small, spun forest
into what will be a girl, the spiderweave of the brain
so fresh nothing has gotten caught to death there yet.
Turn over, aim hand to mouth, miss again. Roll over.
Dead leaves under which so much grows, not yet fruited
out on the vine. Everything seed and dirt in the constant rain,
brush of dead starlight on surface of old ocean.

Self-Portrait at Two and a Half

Kill the new baby brother! Find the candy!
Why can't the talking ever stop?
A fountain of words spraying everywhere.
"Enough already!" the mother's favorite phrase,
along with "Shut up! I can't take it anymore!"
But how can quiet be? The whole world—
the pull puppy with sad eyes, the red magic marker
she chewed on too long, the way so much toilet paper
goes up, not down—made into something else
in the boxcars of words. Meanwhile, the crib gets all
the good stuff: floating animals and bounties of affection,
praise for curls and sleep, gurgling and pooping,
but she has something new too:
a hand-held mirror, and in it, eyes that say,
seeing is not enough.

Self-Portrait at Nine

The rock-n-roll band included the beloved fourth grade teacher,
a tambourine, the cute boy on bass who looked like Ringo,
and the sexy feel of drumsticks in her small gripping palms,
not that she knew how to drum, but sitting, surrounded
by circles of silver appealed immensely, not to mention
the gorgeous obnoxious curves of the noise.
At night, lying awake under giraffe sheets
with a flashlight and Cousin Brucie on AM radio,
she toured with that band, an endless series
of adorations and fine hot cocoas in dimly lit diners.
When she ran, fully awake, down the block in mid-day,
late for the bus, she soared into yet another award,
evidence that you-are-loved-no-matter-what,
her hungry arms and legs running toward this dream
on the speed of bruises charting the silence.

Self-Portrait as Oldest Child

There was a long white tablecloth luminous as skin
enveloping the dining room table and its sexy legs.
In there, she thought the best thoughts.

When the sun came back, she crept to her bed
undaunted as the houseplant leaves shielding
her friends, the pigeons, on the ledge.

Sometimes rain. Sometimes cold.
The sky turned over, blocking the sun for days.
She hated that and so especially lived under
the table, careful of the slick black pumps or loafers

that legged up into adults, so busy with their hands
and mouths above, they didn't notice
the village. They didn't hear the words

she carved her stories into, trying to make sense
of knowing one small place well enough.
She didn't hear their voices rising in animal fear,

the porcelain serving bowl thrown into the wall
just before someone ran upstairs to cry.
She listened instead to the architecture

of the table's underbelly, the thick shag of broken things,
the flittering of her smart hands as they flew
and landed, tucked like old, experienced birds
under her elbows as the house tilted
and rocked her to sleep.

Self-Portrait as Grown-Up

They said this would happen.
Clothing would stay and not go. Cars
would break down or hit other cars.
Boys would become men, and men would not
return calls. Sex would become a declaration,
then a sport, then a minefield, then not anything
static enough to be named. Touch would be too much
or not enough, what to wear would be as existential
as weeding gardens or jump-starting cars, and
dark chocolate would eclipse milk chocolate.
In the morning, she would become the waker-upper
instead of the one woken. In the afternoons,
coffee would be needed along with many distractions
falling across the rooms and cubicles like
early autumn leaves. Money would change
from something needed for the swim club
to a magician's hat that never holds enough rabbits.
Dusk would become night, dishes would be done
or heavy with remnants of animated conversations.
But dreams wouldn't move out of the child house,
a dead father would still be arguing with her
that she said something she didn't and wouldn't,
and when awake again, walking down the street,
stopping to lean on a tree to tie her wild shoelace,
she would still be all the concentric circles at once.

Self-Portrait at Twenty-Five

All the fives that can multiply themselves,
a sex bed of ages creating this one, and this single day,
the morning of her wedding actually. Before the pink
supposed-to-be-dusty-rose gown, the elegantly wrapped pile,
and many people only remembered later by the photos,
there was the sandbar at the river, three friends,
the short walk, the cold bottoms of feet and sunlight
before the falling into the crowded dream of what we call
a momentous occasion, and then into the dark and
day to come, one person, his weight patterning
the sheets like sand, showing that something invisible
passed through here, ready to multiply like
happy cells, sad cells, into what the river
meets around the bend.

Self-Portrait as Pond

I turn my back and a million wings
shiver across my surface. I stop
but the beveling echo doesn't.
I float a half-brown leaf as if
I'm made of open hands.
I hold myself quiet where
the sand parts, each molecule
a tiny ocean, and the old fish sleep
cooled by the blank sheets of
my moving bottom. Nothing not
in motion, I'm as fearless as
the weather I mirror and distort.
I'm as rough as any old fighter
half asleep who jolts up swinging.
Don't cross me. I can outrun you
even in the stillest air and all the
trembling swirls on white fire.
I eat wind and breathe out crossing
angles of passing memory. Don't forget
I am perfectly set in the center
of whoever you think you are.

Self-Portrait at Forty-Two

If the sweater fits, wear it. Otherwise,
a t-shirt. Just anything to cover
the bra, the torso, no longer
churning cells into fetuses
or blood into milk. Wear a coat too,
at least a sweatshirt. You just
never know about the weather.
The sky just a wide exhalation
of love, and love another word for what
is turning into memory, right now,
before our eyes. The what-will-come-next
dizzying in its pattern of ice and broken branch
at eye level outside the kitchen window.
Meanwhile, the luxury of warm water,
the dish sleek as a baby's bottom,
the drain leading all that debris
into the middle of the big field
that, come spring, will light up
in the rushing love of grass.

Self-Portrait as Bodhisattva

How did I get this good? I mean, my goodness
even melts butter into toast that I lovingly feed
the first homeless man sleeping outside
Weaver's Department Store, my enlightened
legs bending gingerly. "Get the fuck away, man!"
Of course I don't take offense, just crumble the bread
and hand-feed it to an injured starling in the alley.
I'm so in love with the world I could evaporate.

Self-Portrait as Fuckhead

You think I don't know I'm a dick?
I got news for you, bub,
self-awareness doesn't just
pave the road to virtue.

Self-Portrait as KitchenAid Mixer

It is the job of a god taking like and not like,
breaking it down into a singular substance.
Sometimes the other attachments—the cheese
shredded, carrots sliced, meat ground, flour
noodled out to delight she-who-feeds me.
Sometimes weeks of hanging out with the
microwave and toaster, friends certainly
but also the ones who see real combat daily,
expose their cores to blinding heat to make
something for the world. I hate them really.
Me, a Swiss Army knife of an appliance, a chameleon
of white and charm, the one who makes them hope
this way of creating could be the righteous pathway
to the good life, I just bide my time, yearn to slum
with the measuring spoons and sexy rubber spatula,
maybe whip a few dozen eggs or turn flour into
a ball of potential around my hook, give myself
a ride into the dervish of my core, the hum of my brain,
my unmoving feet beautiful in their exact stillness.

Self-Portrait as Hand

I tell fortunes, the lines in me extinct
talismans. It's really the muscles
that lift and open the world,
apple by apple. I'm not afraid
of my strength, the engine souls
of my palms, the curling and
uncurling fingers you depend on
without noticing. I'm wizened as
an old tree, spiffy as a happy tool.
I'm holding things or taking them,
falling on the keys, aiming toward
ignition, leaning on an arm
or leaping to his waist when
no one's looking.
I'm good-looking too,
never too fat or ill-clad,
loopy as a cocktail party,
sporting my wedding band
like a loose bone.
When you stop mostly all the
other limbs and muscles, I'm still
agile as apples, happy as
the day is long, holding all
that can't be held
without dropping a word.

Self-Portrait as Ecstasy

Always so generous, wanting
to give itself, like plush bouquets
of deep red peonies that stand at
the dark end of a room
and explode.

Like the ceiling fan
that serves without complaint.
Like the sky out west
beyond mountains.
Like rain that forgets
it was here yesterday
then halts into clean twilight.

Happy as antelope running,
happy as flies on the watermelon rinds,
happy as the sleeping dog
under the table in summer.

A freshly painted bluebird-blue chair
once old. Happy as a nail doing its job,
or my hands in warm water, cleaning
the last dish after all the friends
have left the feast, the silence
itself a form of ecstasy, or what song
it makes when it sings in chorus.

Self-Portrait for Day-Long Life

for Barry and Robin

I opened my fist, small as
a carnation, only blue, transparent.
My round eyes marveling
at the legs that raced over,
a nurse's hand along the side
of my body trying to steady
the trembling of my heart.

Of course I knew their voices—
my mother, my father, their tones
as what I dreamt trees were,
a dance of inflection that held
the moving globe of my old home
before this—piercing cries
of machines that sadden my bones,
other voices, the moving dots
and lights of a face I do not know
brought into focus by a smell
that's home, that housed
my dive from cell to cell, the
swirling clatter of the spine
lengthening, the happy tide
of brain and trembling limbs
so suddenly out of flight
and heat to here where the air
hurts my lungs, where the tunnel
of blackbirds I cannot see
powers over the skylight
breaking down the sun
into warm rain,
and I'm gone.

Self-Portrait at Sixty

What a big balance of numbers,
6 x 10, 4 x 15, 2 x 30, 3 x 20
so much to divide into the body
of seasons, hauntings, calm skies.
What is happening already? Why does memory
freshen itself only as an unexpected guest
who then tosses furniture in the street?
So much more to listen to now that
the listening has begun. She walks the first
grandchild late at night, his breath on her cheek,
counting itself into her hair. She remembers
the first pregnancy, how she couldn't stop counting.
Then in labor, she knew why—a tag for each breath,
a way to hold pain and walk memory to come.
Oh, great tulip tree of the yard!
Oh, happily moving white car!
Let her walk and count, hold the speeding
tremor between breaths so vast behind her
it's as if she's lived infinity.

Self-Portrait as Insomnia

Hush, little babies, lie gentle on your tummies.
Sleep when I scratch your backs.

Don't roll over and weep, not again.
What hasn't happened isn't going to happen.

No shame in that.
Stop trying so hard. Stop trying

hard enough. You think you know
what's enough? You don't.

Calm, little babies. What is it
you need from me, whose milk dried?

What love do you need?
The bed is firm enough for sleep.

The pillow cool as snow melt from a high place
that traveled a season to get here.

What is there to cry about?
The dark holds you tenderly as purple irises.

Self-Portrait at Eighty

Is she alive like paper now, or more like an
old dolphin, and what of the sudden waves of
nausea, the weakness in each knee, the way all the parts
that bend struggle to hold their range of motion?
While there might be phone calls that make her happy,
messages that come from long-ago bottles tossed
into the pale breeze of a March day, what is turning
green at its center? Will all the answers be worn down
to their gears by the time she finds out, the questions curling
around her like decades-old blankets even when she sits,
just like she did as a girl, on the rock, leaning into
the scent of Asiatic lilies making her think
she isn't human any more, or at least, not just.

Self-Portrait as Woman Who Loves Her Body for a Moment

My ankles, for instance, functional
as bicycle pedals, the elbows too,
elegant as the unfurling of an iris.
Then there are my thumbs, twin sons
of a mother who never forgets them,
marvelous in their gymnastics.

My eyes that land on orange in a painting,
or my shoulders, heroic in their lifting.
The flat slate of blue crooked lines where
there used to be breasts, the curve of my belly,
the hips weary of insults when they surge
across the days like prize-winning horses.
The way my knees bend to make strong hills
of the legs. Then there's the hummingbird synapses
of my brain, tired but as lovely in their blur
as the heart's tap dance and dramatic bows.

Everywhere, there's applause my white blood cells
drink each leg of their marathon, the efficiency
of my tongue, the wind my lungs translate into song,
and the fire at the center of each breath.

In the mirror, walking through foot-high snow,
or turning to sit in the chair, this body's imperfections
just the weather rolling through the landscape of the soul.
Why insult the thick heat, the broken branches that left
their lines, the dappled rocks up close?
I'm just a container for time like a river.
Tell, me, what's not to love?

Self-Portrait as Wind

It's always like this. Or it isn't.
Moon or its influence under cloud. The pull
of dirt into the center. The drop
in temperature that glides open
the ground, the spark, the disappearance
of light. All of this and me
or none of it. But give me a palette
of grass, or the shimmering coiled tops
of trees. Give me rain or heat,
the slice of space between skyscrapers,
the way wings make me, and I make wings,
weather too. Give me nothing
and I'll use it. Give me weight
and I'll drop it. The swish of a
mare's tail. The buzz of a confused wasp.
The rush of a man running against me,
into me, trying to make time. I make
the opposite of time. Fortunes just paper,
and you know what I do to that.
Blinds unbound. Geese scattered
over the next hill of air, everything falling back
into my large hands, me who can't
hold onto a thing.

Jubilee

Are you ready to give it all up, the news
that isn't news, the sullen child calling the shots,
the scared grip of the fingers, the longing
of the spine? Are you ready to step out
into this new life, naked in the night rain?
Will you bring here the supposed treasures—
lost boys buried in cigar boxes, a glass bird
perched on the window box, the earnest wish
for someone to change her mind about you?

Jubilee is not all dance and fall.
Get up from that curb where you wait
for the parade of acceptance or the
nightmares of fear. Your life is not
made of the nameable.

The party has already started,
only a small flame that catches it all:
paper, rages, old shoes, miscarriages, empty
medicine bottles and torn blankets.
The fire that, once invited, consumes itself
and makes warmth for you, sitting there
in your new skin.

Now find or make another house.
Whatever comes, give away.
Don't wait for answers from authority,
don't push choices before their time.
Stand on the threshold, looking out,
imagining how one small bulb,
the size of dead newborn rabbit,
once in the ground, can winter itself
into the power of hyacinth.
Don't settle for anything less.

The Road Is Just a River

for Kelley

Listen to how the old pain no longer
beats its low drums for you to try harder.
Instead there is the window open
and the air sweet in its silence
and leaf fall. What is this for, your life?
A wavering of desire and gratitude,
a hot number yearning to be picked,
an old lily, open and dying? A story
opening wider each day as you take in
the horizon, and let the horizon take in you.

The wind aches, the waters trill in ocean or bathtub.
You hold your stomach in your sleep
and hope for a dream merciful enough
to carry you the whole night and next day too.
What song are you singing yourself toward now
with the fullness of all the grief
and joy your body knows,
through the pages of your story at this moment?

The fire in the corner holds.
All the old fear or grief that once clothed you
sits on the chair, nothing that fits anymore.
The weather you thought you knew
is all birth again. Sunflowers fill
the field, following the daily passion
for light face to face. You wake up
and take your first step into
the new story you're walking,
the old road a shimmering river.

Five-Year Anniversary at the Grand Canyon

"You're cured," says the date as it tumbles
over the night and stands upright.
So you wake and open the motel door
into a parking lot herded by ponderosa pines.
More steps, past the cafeteria brimming with
young Thai women mastering chicken-fried steak,
there's a sidewalk. A large woman in a wheelchair
is pushed toward her car. The train tracks,
seemingly delicate in their hold of seven deer
and the flowers on which they graze,
then the drop off you'd expect,
but larger, enough so as to hold
the sorrow of a billion dying birds.

It is nothing to toss a coin of a wish
from this height where wishes never fall directly
but catch in the trembling weather
of assorted circumstance and whatever
cross breeze is made by the wind
you hear only in the stillest sleep.

Your happy hand on the railing
between the tour bus and SUV,
and the flipping upside down of space
into this arrival, a small grace,
a tender place to hold onto
now that you actually see
what rivers do to rock.

That Tree Is a Genius

You can see it in the way it lets
wind pour through one side of branches
without tiring itself, all bend.
How it leans and then lets the sun
pull it closer. How it drags a jubilee of leaf,
stepping out of itself without going anywhere.

Put your hand on its trunk.
Feel the pulse of no pulse,
the legs that shot up decades ago
from roots that ran like rivers
around rock and slope, through
lives that leave no remnant.
That tree holds it all,
sees who we love best
and why we despise ourselves too often.

Loves the change in the weather
which is always, holds mountains
of birds ascending and flying away.
That whole tree sings its mourning dove
then sings wind, a genius of history
and branch crossings, a dancing fool
all winter. That tree is my body.

I Would Touch You

Like a crow landing on cedar branch, wavering
like breath in the winter. Or like the underside
of a rabbit, sleeping. Or even like water rushing
to catch up with itself between the weary banks.

I would make my hands like leaves falling
or loose ribbons of water, like a fish flying upstream
in a frenzy of blue and black.
My eyes would sing tree root and distilled light
across the rising dust filtering the air between us,

telling you, touch me here
where our sight is so clean that
each blade of grass, each tilted branch
stands in relief against the fast, slow backdrop
of what we call time or death.
Let me touch you where it's all true.

Alive

for the people in my serious illness writing groups

They said you wouldn't be here by now,
but here you are, writing of one red bird
that shot through the fog like an arrow on fire.

Some of you with hands that tremble
and forget how much gravity to give
the paper, some of you with sonograms
of small shadows in the wrong place.
All with stories that crest the heights:
a falling-down fence and abandoned homestead,
the detail of fern against a mailbox, a daughter in
her wedding gown, a son long gone, and a photo
of you a year after diagnosis, standing at the rim
of the Grand Canyon, the air lit
from the long drop behind you.

Statistics are meaningless against these stories
that lead you, stone by stone, to your own breath
hot and vital, alive and cellular with memory,
with the daring to imagine how you arrived here
alive.

In the End, There Is Only Kindness

for Gene

When the floor slips and the time comes,
when interventions falter, there is only kindness,
a lantern to hold at journey's end, then hand over
so someone else can lift the light enough
to illuminate where to step next, and how.

In this kindness, there are always stories:
Telling the checker who rang up his milk twice,
don't worry, everyone makes mistakes.
His long wait among aging magazines at the VA
so a homeless vet could get his medication.
Gravel on our walkway because he didn't want
us slipping when we brought home the new baby.
Jokes about being old and decrepit while he
cooked everyone dinner. How he power-rocked
the babies to sleep, his heart beating through theirs.
Christmas stockings and grandchildren to wake up early,
coins to collect for each one. Oxygen in one hand,
a cane in the other so he could see a grandchild
in orchestra or band, graduation or swim meet
even when his back and memory hurt.
The dishes or long drives, reaching for the check,
and taking the time to greet the stranger eating alone.
Only kindness matters in the circle of love
he made out of this world.

In the end, there is always the beginning,
a seamless turn from here to there
even if everything is different from
the irreplaceable loss shining and aching at once,
a kind of river running alongside our lives,
or weather reminding us that
we love, were loved by a man here only
for kindness, which is not just a kind of love
but the only love there is.

Daniel's Dream Speaks

For Daniel I stoop slightly,
stretch out my wings
and launch across that divide to show him
cattle grazing in multiples of seven,
dramas of kings played out in garments and famines,
sweet figs hollowed with dry heat to leather.

Listen, boy, I tell his open ear.
He turns toward me, eyelashes on his cheeks.
Daylight rips aside the sweet darkness.

Meanwhile, lions curl at his feet with no fear
and god naps close to his forehead.
He dreams of women with browned skin
and lips like small, unopened roses
who gather in the sallow field
arm in arm, singing to the clouds.

What do you see now, Daniel,
I ask as the squawking near my black eyes fades.
He rolls back into sleep, determined to hold
this remembering against the taut mouth
of men and women everywhere hungry for the kind of sleep
that answers questions by showing children
running among trees into the next
jubilee of forgiveness.

Prayer for the Moment of Change

Let what will happen happen:
The end of the month I counted out 10 days ago
is here. The mosquitoes move on. Hard freeze
in a land of one big thing and infinite little ones.

Let the blue of sky, green of leaf, rust of grass,
fall like specks of dust. Let me walk through
the change faded with age, among the drought-scarred
and dead wrappings of another time.

Let the sky, never one to resist change, show
its clever hand in snow that doesn't amount to much,
or worn light of December balancing between sundogs.

Let the dark come, and a revelation of stars
cut clear when the cold erases the veil. Let me stand there
and watch, in the shouts of nothing from nothing,
the night a black stone under ice.

Let the feathering begin, let the soft blue
that would never hurt anyone show its teeth,
and the river, someplace north of here,
thicken its speech until it has nothing to say.

Let the tip of death into life, water to ice,
make a new place to be.

Your Heart Has No Gate

No fenceposts to hang a gate from either,
nothing even to enclose. How can you hold the wind
when it sweeps through the stubble field of your sorrow?
What belongs here as opposed to there?

Don't you see, little sister, old father,
boy on the brink of man, small child,
that there never was, never could be an actual way
to hold back, not from this sweet motor of synapse
and fire that turns you toward the moment arriving
in each breath. Don't you already know that
your life is a flock of birds filling every branch
on the windswept cedar?

The scraps of lumber you place here, or how
you stay far back from the borderland
does not make an actual gate. A comfort maybe
but no gate. The vigorous gymnastics
of your thoughts lift and propel you, but still,
the heart trembles in its nest; takes in, releases
all your blood every four minutes;
releases itself into the stippled blues and greens
of the awakening world. It knows no other truth
than what it makes when you acknowledge
there's nothing to protect, but everything to save.

Landed

Here everything is a list of its details:
the surface of crow feather where it bows,
or echo of whippoorwill through the closed window
over the bed. The chiggers and the slow-creeping
cedar trees, milkweed webbed with spittlebug,
and the grass above and below ground,
mirroring out from a single point
of root and longing.

I'm landed here, in the center of something
not my own doing, and although I keep thinking
I'm alone, I'm dying, I'm afraid,
I'm making all that up.
The man I love is coming out of the woods,
the long crescent of his body closer, bowing to touch
something, say its name.

When he stands back up, he walks slowly to show me
whatever we think of love is just the aerial view
that tells us nothing compared to the soft green stems
that curl and fall with the wind, compared to how
each step across the grass is a form of falling
out of and into what losses make life possible.
The quick flashes, like the sun balancing
on the lip of the horizon right before
it goes out, like that moment the field golds
everything opaque, like how love strips us
out of the stories we have for love.

The Last Moment

On the corner, the accordion player
infuses the humid night with a darkness
sweet and grieving in perfect hue
with the green neon fish two stories up, over the bar,
you crossing the street, a nighthawk diving,
and the cobalt blue of the sky, almost turquoise
at the edges of a leafy horizon.

This is your town on a hot June night.
You reach the other side, turn away
from the swaying musician and tattered linden tree.
Down the block, you see only one room lit
at the top of the loft apartment building;
in that room, a potted ficus tree and a chair
someone may or may not be sitting in.
You turn toward the alley, aim yourself
between decay and limestone,
stairs on one side, blue dumpster on the other.
A breeze pours down from the rooftops, and
you realize this could be the last moment
you remember, decades from now, as you lean
into death or stop leaning away.

This could be the line between the life you've lived
and the life you will live as you step across
the parking lot, toward your husband and sons,
already in the car with the new books
you will have long read and forgotten
by the time this is a memory,
by the time so many you love are gone,
so many you don't yet imagine are here.

You reach for the car door to join
the present, the blue chord of your life,
the pulse of time and music,
the quick fire, the wide water of home.

Reading the Body

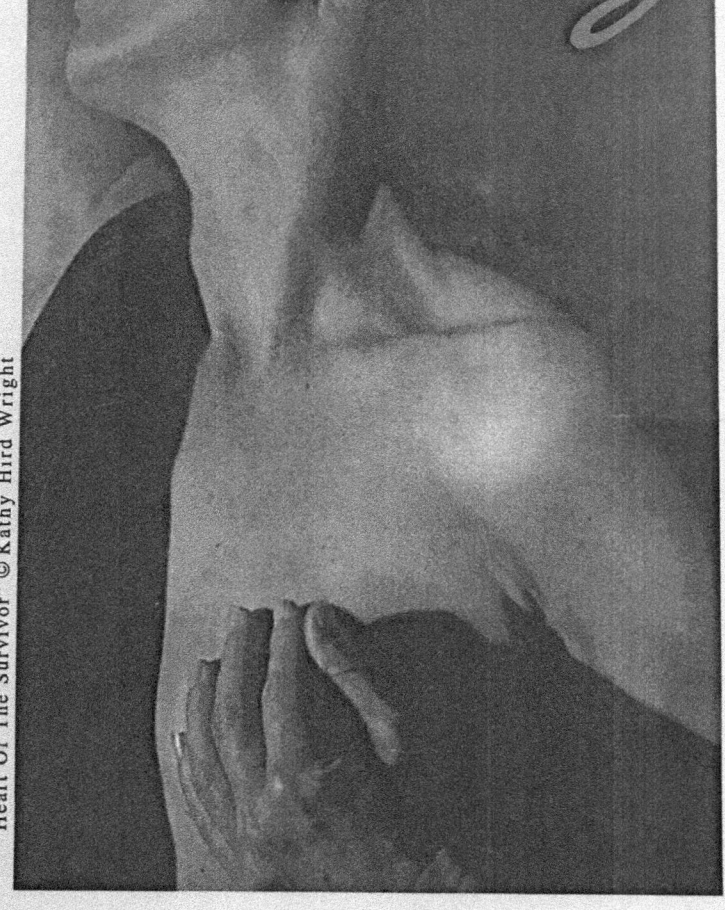

"Heart Of The Survivor" © Kathy Hird Wright

by Caryn Mirriam-Goldberg

Discovering Fire

I have discovered fire—
a tiny flame in my left breast,
miniature in its heat,
asymmetrical and hungry as it tilts
toward the lymph nodes.

When the surgeon lifted it out
so that it could be magnified
into the blue core of its heat,
someone else also lifted the small flame
from my body, cupped it in her hands,
carried it up the hill to the wide savannah
before she fed it into a burning bush.

Now, not so far from that windy place,
I watch my husband cup the plastic bag
of red chemo in his hands, bless it,
return it to the nurse.
Now, not so far from the heat of this,
we pray for the embers
in my blood stream to turn to ash,
dissolve into underground rivers.

At the same time, along the shorelines,
all the ones I have ever loved
sit at their campfires in the dark
as I'm swept past, as I try to swim again
back to a time before I discovered fire,
back to a place that has turned
into someplace else.

Diagnosis

Not what you'd expect, not in this ordinary body:
the phone message on the machine that says,
"mammogram" and "irregular," the technician's voice
later who tells you there's something
to look at, make sure, check, just in case.

Then it's that moment alone in the bedroom,
the chair so large and forgiving, the panic that suddenly
seems extraterrestrial, the incessant questions
while the wait stretches its beginning to meet you.

Until the second x-ray hangs on the lit box
singing out its small constellation of calcium, until the
surgeon's receptionist touches your shoulder kindly
and nods, until you lie on a still table
while a nurse looks, shrugs just a little,

until that call, and those words which come
by the time you already know them, you
already know the walls of your body falling away,
this dropping down to your seat, to your notebook
where you write it down because you're supposed to,
to your fingers looking so normal
as they hold the pen and paper, unfurling

this new script, this open page
of a body where, without moving an inch,
you've become a flesh-and-bones double
of who you always were—one who has cancer,
one who can't believe it, and both of you
standing up, shaking the hand of the doctor,
walking out into widest sky you've ever seen.

Morning Glory

Blue as blue light, silk against sky,
and you can only look at them
with that deep knowing that something
is wrong, something asleep for years
wakes your life with a jolt.

At night, you ask yourself, where do
the morning glories go in the dark,
the ones that widen open in such purple,
such blue, such pink that seems
to be the definition of those colors?
Who do they bloom for in their dreams
with no trace of nightmare or forgetfulness?

You think of these flowers all around and
far away too, closed tightly and carefully
while you are open wide
to this small reverse blossoming
in your own breast. You dream of
morning glories climbing all the fences,
morning glories poured over steps
and ledges, even this one
where you wait to see
what will happen to you.

The Landscape of the Body

There are heights here I never noticed before—
bare rock I grip, my knuckles gleaming
as I pull myself up, trembling and breathing hard
until I can steady the scared soul
in the calm pool of the body.

I never noticed how much light inhabits this place
or the slim fingers of walnut leaves feathering
over the hidden birch, the singular palm tree
growing anyway in a cold climate,
the dance of cloud reflected
in a distant buildings' wall of mirror.

I never noticed how small I am against the rock,
and how the rock is in the ocean of sky.
How miniature my heartbeat, and at the same time,
how loud the cacophony of hope and fear

while everywhere birds dive toward dinner,
and my bones sing
to what makes stars visible.

Already

When we climbed the hill in April, a cool night,
almost wet, windless so that the candle I carried
didn't waver, when we climbed half-way up to a small
clearing, an old tree, you with your shovel,
me with my poems and prayers, when we climbed
to this very spot where you'd dig, I'd read the poems
thanking my breasts, say the prayers for safe passage
through surgery, easy surrender, full recovery,

the loss had already began,
the breasts falling from me were already
in motion, and what would be left,
who I would be next,
already a mystery

so that the next day, waking from anesthesia,
and the next, going home and walking a short distance
to gather lilac with sore arms, and the next week,
lying on damp ground to carefully place
the salvia and statis in the prepared soil

were all part of the same story beginning long ago,
before cancer or even my life, of how each shovel
into the earth to plant something, each seed,
each word, each moment
of silence or rain or cloud light

is simply how blossoms must storm through darkness.

Lilac

The day after they cut my breasts off,
just home from the hospital, not even
napping or talking on the phone yet,
that day, I walked on my own two legs
down the dirt road over the slope of loose rocks,
cradling, as I walked, the broken body,
the large orange handled clippers, the big wind
holding me, the man I loved behind me getting ready
to start his car to come get me, that day beginning
the healing from all of it—unslashed from the expectation
of what knife or infusion comes next

was the day I made my way to my mother-in-law's
old-fashioned dark purple lilac, and reached against
the tightness of gauze and paper tape, against
the odd sensation of parts removed and scars
just making themselves, against my sore arms reaching
toward their old strength

to gather and hold, to cut and cut and cut
all I could fill my arms with, all the dark purple
alive with death and birth, loss and blossom,
and the white ones too.

My arms filling with the explosion of lilac,
my life filling with wind and weight of branches,
all of it against, upon, my open chest,
all of it ready to be carried
into the next life
that starts right now.

What Do You Want To Remember?

The way my hand could tunnel into the soft dirt
at twilight. The plant I couldn't see clearly,
and how it felt to press the baby dirt around it.
The cool air as I turned on the hose.
The beautiful arc of soft water shining down
on the garden like lamplight.

I want to remember always how my son squints
when he says, "Mom, how's the cancer going?"
the quiet breathing of his question just before exhaling,
the garden in the dark we look at together.
The sharp light from the house of cats and dirty dishes.

The way the earth opens to put in seeds.
The way the night opens for 2 a.m. storms
to pass through unnoticed. The way the house
opens for dreams to fly into us as we sleep.
The opening of eyes still half in those dreams,
trying to plant one life into another.

Breastless

I stood in front of the mirror bare-chested,
a flat slate, open field, horizonless
like the round earth isn't really
so round anymore.

The slim trails of stitches, crooked line
that climbs a little, dives a little
across each side. The branding
in my clavicle where chemo port went in,
chemo port came out, the almost
invisible pink line in the left armpit
in lieu of lymph nodes there, and
the ruddy thicker line down my stomach
to pubic bone, dividing belly into two halves—

all the parts exposed, slashed expertly open,
all these parts surrendering their goods
to the surgeon's hands, sealing themselves
back up like the earth cut open, excavated,
re-landscaped to accommodate new clearings,
the mining for danger and risk,
the yearning for long life.

I stood in front of this mirror
while the moon hung soft and round
in the corner of the bathroom window,
while the kids argued in the other room
over the clashing tones of television,
while the cat slept on my bed just beyond,
while the bathwater roared into its container
soon ready to part and let me in,
and I knew it was still the same place—
the same grasslands, butterfly milkweed,
the same storms parading over—
of my body.

All the skin complete,
all the blood complete,
all the muscle complete,
all the tears, all the breathing
ongoing toward this completeness,
and all of it, beyond understanding, good.

Your Life is Your Life

Know this when you must lie
completely still on the steel table
while the glass plate presses down
on your chest. Your life
obviously your life. Dream it back
into your memory for when
the kool-aid-colored chemo
is pumped into the plastic port
in your clavicle. Tell yourself
this when the doctor comes in
to talk with you, carrying
a small box of tissues. Don't
forget then how your life is
your life, not when the phone rings
at the wrong time, or the biopsy needle
inserted in your left breast shoots
its click near your heart. Your life beats
loud and often. Your life
surges against itself
in at least some cells so tell it
your life is your life
when you sit, naked from
the waist up on the examining table.
Your life there talking with
the pharmacist or here on the couch
is your life. Pick it up
and hold it close
especially when the wait
is long and the news is bad.
Tell your life what it is.

I Want to Tell You How Beautiful You Are

I want to tell you how beautiful you are
with your flat chest soaring
into scar across your heart and lungs.
I want to tell you even this is beautiful,
and even the rounded flesh below, the silhouette
hollowed here, extended there, the shapes new
and sudden, the beauty you could never see
when they cut your body open to where
the breathing organs breathe, the beauty
you'll mourn from the other side of your life.

I want to tell you, believe this now,
stop doubting that because it's not
what you wanted, what you expected,
it's not beauty. It is

just like weather you didn't expect,
just like ground cut back to hold more
perennials and wider swatches of
the wildest grasses.

It may not be pretty but I want you
to finally believe, now on the far side of girlhood,
past growing and giving birth to three children,

and now while you can still open and hold him,
his hands praising your re-grown hair
and flat new chest
that you are, beyond belief
and inside it too,
beautiful.

Reading the Body

I am still a woman
even if my whole chest aches
with emptiness, my soul shakes
because this body was cut,
one part off another.

In the tree, a dark bird with a red chest,
small, trembling, looks side to side.
The cedar boughs shake,
the cottonwood leaves too
while the soft edge of the horizon
watercolors into rain to come.

Is this where I live?
The absence of sun.
My chest empty. Breasts flown away.
I want them back. They want me back.
A lover's tangle in water and blood.
A choice based on a bet
that this gives me a clearer shot
at long life.

So much to carry on this chest
where knives lived and needles,
where small birds nested,
where trees blossomed,
where silence sang
in the voice of water,
where lands landed—holding
what was there, spanning the open
space to read this
new Braille of the body.

Playing the Cello

The soul knows grief
so I play the cello,
hold the bow like a wand
that must dip into sound,
connect with the tender steel
of the string in just the right way,
my shoulder relaxing,
my forearm extending,

I hold this cello, its torso
the size of my torso,
its neck close to my neck,
its hips between my legs.
I hold it close and do something
I've never done before
each time I try.

Somewhere in the emptiness
it shapes and holds,
there is a song
made of wind and forest.
There is a body, my body,
fragile as music or time.
There is a long call low
as that darkness just at the edge
of dawn, bright as that almost
turquoise blue before the late night.

I balance the bow and press the song
into the grief that knows this music too.

Bridges

All that year of cancer and surgeries,
of my father's cancer and death as I held
his knee, of his chemo and mine,
long waits for injections or test results,
I dreamt of bridges—large suspension bridges
I had to scale with my hands or climb over
gingerly with trembling legs.
Slim wooden slats stories above certain
rocks, and always a slat or two
missing in the high wind. Crossing
expansive spaces made of water
or shifting ground, junkyards or rivers,
untold distances to master.

Sometimes there were ways to stop climbing—
a phone call or a plane ticket, another needle
in my forearm, the gleaming ceiling of the
waiting room while the magazine spread itself
across my lap, telling me of other destinations.
Or there was the occasional fall as I sat on the bed,
the fear storming through me like shards
of nightmare, the reaching out for help
from that sensation of going under.

I do not have words big enough for how far I traveled.
I do not have language intimate enough
for how I arrived here, to the world more itself
than it ever was before, tender as the last breath
of my father, fierce as the woman
waking up again on the other side.

Animals in the House

poems by

Caryn Mirriam-Goldberg

Girl

When I was a girl I didn't know
I was a girl. I thought I was
more of a pigment, a choral tone,
some kind of weather that disrupts
everyone's life in the living room.
I knocked over the cast iron iron again,
and this time it broke. How could
you break an iron iron? they yelled,
but how could I not? The weight of
metal on the earth, wanting to return.
When money was missing, I thought surely
I must have taken it.
When it rained, a hurricane this time,
I thought, see what you've done now.
I didn't believe in cause and effect, elements of
surprise, or the slim chance meetings
that changed everyone's lives. I didn't know
that people were supposed to end,
contained as vases to hold
whatever you gave them.

I thought we were more like land, islands even,
unfurling in the brown haze of the sea.
I thought there was water everywhere,
pouring us into changeable shapes—
leaf or puppy or branch. All falling
toward wherever we came from
not afraid or surprised,
not bad or tricked into good.

All falling back into the horizons that come
each evening to meet the fire.

Magnolia Tree in Kansas

This is the tree that breaks
into blossom too early each March,
killing its flowers. This is the tree
that hums anyway in its pool of fallen
petals, pink as moonlight. Not a bouquet
on a stick. Not a lost mammal in the clearing
although it looks like both with its explosions
of rosy boats—illuminated, red-edged.
Not a human thing but closer to what we might be
than the careful cedar or snakeskin sycamore.
It cries. It opens. It submits. In the pinnacle
of its stem and the pits of its fruitless fruit,
it knows how a song can break the singer.
In the brass of its wind, it sings anyway.
Tree of all breaking. Tree of all upsidedown.
Tree that hurts in its bones and doesn't care.
Tree of the first exhalation
landing and swaying, perfume and death,
all arms and no legs. Tree that never
learns to hold back.

Tricks of Gravity

What was surprising was the quiet.
The neighborhood in twilight, the blood
coming out some part of my face,
even the streetlights so familiar
as if I hadn't just crashed into a row of cars.
Honeysuckle the only sound
through the open windows of my car.
Just like longing, I knew then,
a scent you want, you want
but lean into and it's gone.

When they pulled me from the car,
said, say your name,
I said yours, wanting so much
I didn't know I was hurt.

Hours later, on the pull-out sofa,
all the bandages in place,
we lay on our sides facing
into that honeysuckle everywhere.
A gravity. An inevitability. I knew
I could never not turn this way,
and if I did, I could never not want more.
A crashing you hear the moment before impact.
So we pressed together once
in that ache that comes
right after an accident when no one knows yet
how much damage gravity does
to the world all the time.

About Desire

1.
Northern lights! So we grab our baby and run north. When we stop, our breath hardening in the air, he says, we made a mistake. It's only fog over the airport lights. But it's still amazing, he lies.

2.
In the good dream I lean my hands on the kitchen table where my great-aunts eat cheesecake with cherries. I squat slightly. Now labor can begin, but instead the baby's head crowns. I pull it out by its shoulders and tell the aunts, it's a girl. Well that was easy, they say, but why aren't you wearing any panties?

3.
Even this far south, in our neighborhood once, with everyone in the middle of the street, TV guides under their arms, pointing up and staring, we saw the red flare across the stars. We saw it move.

4.
In the bad dream a man with food in his beard says, it's a miscarriage. He spits tobacco on the floor, whispers, and it's your fault.

5.
Desire is like dust, the bodhisattva in the bathroom says. Put it in a certain light, it becomes what you yearn for.

Dust on the atmosphere and you get northern lights, an illusion of the divine when really god forgot to vacuum.

6.
Sometimes I go for walks with the baby and his stroller. While he points to every light fixture and says, moon, I feed him the cherries I just bit the pits from. He points to cats and laughs because they're all his. We're happy.

7.
Once, almost asleep, I wanted a lover so much I invented one: tall, muscular, brown hair and blue eyes, all compassionate so he weeps into my hair for my loneliness. This is what Jesus must be like, I thought, but then again, why not the best?

8.
I sit on the grass and cry. The sky is clear, relentless with stars, the grass dry and noisy. He lays out his jacket and unbuttons his jeans. The first baby's asleep, he whispers, let's make another.

9.
In the worst dream I live alone in a tenement, eating soup from the can, cold, and watching reruns of *The Beverly Hillbillies*. I want nothing.

10.
Last week the stomach flu made me lay down and watch flutters of white leaves fall. The train's whistle every half hour turned into an all-knowing animal who would answer any question I had of the universe. After all the aspirin in the house I still couldn't stand it so I got up and vacuumed.

11.
In the best dream of all I'm awake and can ask anything: what is god? may I have an orgasm now? am I pregnant? make cheesecake materialize. And the answer—always the same—is a picture of the planet with a red arrow pointing to a glob of green next to a sign flashing, yes, you are here.

Leap

The light around the tree returns
 to say it never left.

It returns to say it sees me
still a girl in a pale yellow dress,
white socks ringed with dirty lace,
black patent leather shoes already scuffed.
There, at the base of a tree
trying to make language
out of the way I move my fingers
to call the light back.

But it never left.
It was only the volume of the world's language
turned up, those flippant slaps accompanied
by rushed vowels and faded patience

while I was caught in the blue rapture
of bird-like shapes of sky
made by leaf bent over branch,
while I was caught dreaming of standing very still
on the third story ledge of an old school
just before I'd leap

into that space between things
words named away from me,
into that world not yet damaged
in my small body.

What I Could Tell

I could name all the pieces of violence—
the kick or slap, the friendly punch.
"Say it again," the therapist says.
I remember this later, lying in the bathtub
watching my arms and legs float in water, so normal.
Do you see how contained I am? How calm
a poem, as if I were writing about
tree limbs in winter covered in ice. Delicate.
Connected to the glass trunk, bone to bone.

I startle awake. Someone behind me. Reflexes
not everyone has anymore or ever.
But that was another time, weighted in
the cells of skin. Smoke in the vein of the bone.
Does it matter that the shelf of sky was blue,
that there was heat right where
the fist imprinted itself on my leg?
Did it happen like a shovel edge into roots,
someone watching, hands around my neck
before I could speak, and I'm dying
all over again?

There was a room with no air, a cringing
inward, the iris already broken from its bulb.
There was a bathtub with a girl covered
in bruises, the door locked hopefully.

She was tired, so tired
she couldn't stay awake
to tell me what really happened.

Happiness

for Daniel

I knew happiness in one continuous motion
the moment the midwife held up a knife and cut me,
everything shining and breaking. There, pressing
against the window, the cottonwoods that would frame
your childhood, rushing toward us in leaf and wind.

In the dark branches skinned white and peeling
I was just like you, clanging all over inside.
"What's wrong with you, you stupid schmuckhead?"
my father would ask. And my mother, "Remember
to try to make friends." I was your age, Daniel,
friendless, so they took me in the taxi
past the singular birches to see my first shrink, trembling
that the first child didn't understand something vital
about how to glance at the world.

What did I need with the world when I had the tree?
Its legs mined the earth for water,
the very book of happiness, opening
up the spine of each rounding leaf.
Then the wind that would not control itself—
always a miracle, a miracle
to watch no matter how long I waited
from my seven-year-old window,
all the bruises on my arms and legs solitary,
the belt my father used for this
demilitarized on the floor. I was actually happy
and nothing could undo that.

I was actually drowning in happiness
for hours, the leaves, but mostly the trunk
that let them go with such generosity
and tenderness, with such faith
that I felt a hand cupping my forehead,

a miracle singing at the window,
hold me throw me hold me against myself;
at the very center of the trunk,
a thousand green eyes
swimming in a school of green fish
back to the rivers
underground.

Overground, you wake and come sit with me
at the window while the trees
link us, hand over hand of the leaf,
into some tangled branch of happiness
shuddering or lifting slightly
at the slightest breath.

The Wishing Tree Talks

Not so hard to lean back against me,
like falling asleep. Like falling off
a cliff but then it was only a dream.
So lean back. Watch how the world looks
from inside my cupped leaves.

What are you waiting for?
The lip of storm to climb over?
Your thoughts to stop?

Sit down. See how the cusp
of my smallest branches
shadows the gray bluebird.
Watch the wind pour across
your crossed legs on its way to me.
Hear the crickets open the air up
with their wound. Lean in.
Nothing outside of yourself
will hurt you here.

What hurts in the folds of valley,
the bare parts, the rocks?
In the torn ledge of hill,
in the black of the black-eyed susans,
in the curl of breath out of the visible?
It is all the earth dreaming itself
at a speed that would toss you off
if it were not for gravity,

so then it's all gravity.
Sit back down. Look at me.
Have you forgotten what you need to forget?

Almost Totality: Partial Eclipse

This is how I would want it between us:
the edges of your hair so separate
from the sky, the muscle
in your forearm so contoured
and distinct from the lanky hill in the distance,
and your words, clearly delineated
from mine, concentrated not on reaction,
but casting a million slivers,

the crow so still in the mowed grass,
the absence of wind, the carved shadow
of a gesture on a parked car,
the face half-turning back
to hold cardboard up to the sky and see
the end of the world
or the beginning.

Your face looking at the sun no longer
so dangerous, past almost totality
as your clothes follow the lines
of your body, the muted grass mats
in the wind, your arm lifts slightly
to touch my back like a tree branch
and I can't tell anything
that makes us separate.

The Dark Between the Stars

Lyra climbs the roof, a splattering of constellation
translated into a shape we can name.
See the teapot of Sagittarius, the Northern Cross,
and that ankle dangling from invisible hooks
in the milky way?

We stand in the yard and point, you behind me,
an oversized shadow of heat and shade.
See the dark between stars where nothing seems to be?
Even there, galaxy piled upon galaxy,
and at the same time, the space between the nothing.
Later, when we can't keep our eyes open anymore,
sleep tumbles over us. A falling open of archway and air,
a phone ringing, then the phone turned into
a cotton sheet flapping outside all night
against the hard sky.

I wake dreaming in multiples of nine that correlate
to lakes spilled across the grid of the Midwest.
The weight of everyone's wounds in a particular town
where the dull pain fountains so smoothly
you don't realize it's pain. Everything rushing apart
in random orange dots, the fibers of the eye,
something that sounds like an owl in the dark,
like the screech of a car

and nothing, not drinking a glass of water
or turning on the light, can keep me from sleeping
right back into this dream of infinity
well below the shapes skies make,
the curve of the forehead
that holds in the brain, the slope
of hill in the distance
that mimics the horizon
so all I can do is wake you, say, tell me

Caryn Mirriam-Goldberg

how to undream this, tell me the names
of these constellations that won't stay
still enough to name.

You fold your legs under my knees,
place your open hand on the side of my face,
and say, the opposite of infinity
is love.

Three Walking Songs for the Night

1.
I walk across a field. No more destination,
journey through or over water.
No more dreams of arriving.

I'm here, overlooking a small slope
that leads nowhere. Leaves drop out
of the wet branches. The field eats them.

A fox. Then the sky turns itself
like a clever hand this way and that,
blocking or letting through the moon.

Sometimes rain falls. No matter.
The animals come anyway.
When it clears, I lie on the fallen grass,
look at the brave sky,
and tell myself, "shut up and trust that."

2.
When I wake in the dark, I will go to the forest
with no flashlight, and walk slowly, afraid,
letting my feet make out where next to step,
waiting for what's hidden to let me into its hiding.
No longer dreaming of his hands cupping my head
tenderly, I will just walk in, feeling only
where to land, the noise of the running world no longer running,
the tree frogs cupping their motor song over
the motor song of the cicadas, the brush of branch
on branch, the owls a broken harmonic.

Oh, dream of being loved so perfectly,
Oh, dream of forgiveness,
Oh, damp moon in a pool of clouds,
wide stillness of nothing that we call sky,
now, please let me be brave enough.

3.
I was afraid most of that year.
No particular reason.
Just the rush of old air through my lungs
as if it had nothing better to do.

I'd wake a lot at night, puppy diving
after the kitten, the baby nightmaring
right into the center of my good dream.
I'd wake for nothing also,

sit up, climb out of bed, walking the house
to prove to myself there was no reason
to be afraid. I mean, look at that moon
carrying itself branch to tree branch.
Look at the indentations the wind makes
of its body in the grass.

See how round the earth is,
remember how many animals sleep
hidden like prayers in the tall grass.

See the open mouth of the sky, the shifting of stars
across the throat of the universe,
this time in its slot actually happening.

Lightning, No Thunder

Across the diagonal of the house
my son sleeps in his own sweat,
a good sign, I tell myself.
A show of fire fleshed through
the pores of the body
after nights of high fever.
"Nothing I can explain," says one doctor.
"It doesn't make sense," says another.
They shrug toward a virus, an animal
not alive, a thing
not dead.

Tonight I sit outside on a bench
in the center of the trembling
sky. Heat lightning all directions
the trees don't mask. Occasionally
a strand of fire pulled down
and under into that far away dirt.

Last night I carried that big
eight-year-old boy to my bed,
all night my hand on his forehead
while the heat charged his skin. But this
is the earth too, the very substance
there asleep in that turning
while I sit right outside his whole life
and ask the sky,
Please.

Burning the Prairie

1.
A field is a black hole, shadow made solid
fastened to the ground.
The skull of a baby deer lies there
in the old black hair.
The closed entrance to a mouse house
in dirt that filters sunlight
like the heart filters blood.
I stand on the field's ledge, think about the past,
charred only where I've touched it.
The stories of one slow burn or another.
How much water is there in the world anyway?

Not enough, says the inside of a cave.
Not enough, says the snippet of lilac in the bedroom.
Not enough, says this field.

2.
Years ago, my husband was burning a field
when the field started burning him back.
Caught in the change of wind
clanging the flames closer so they could do
what they long to do most their whole fire life
—rush up a huge sheet of brilliance—
he did the only thing to save his life:
he ran through the fire.

3.
A duck cries. I dream I'm standing
in the burned field again, but before it was burned.
I don't like all this tangle and height.
I want the future cleared away,
absent and present at once.

4.
We burn the field so the grass
can have its house back,
clean out the houseguest-from-hell trees,
sweep the floors, open the windows
to let the smoke out.

We burn the field so that we, ignorant to the black sky,
can see sheet after wavy sheet of burning,
and call it beauty.

We burn the field to start something we can't stop,
and then stop it.

5.
After the burn, I hold my husband's hand
in the bedroom like it's a candle
I wouldn't want to tip toward
all that dry, all that's above ground.

No one talking, the dark as heavy
inside as it is out, the ceiling fan swooshing
us still. I am scared to lie here with the wind
so high, the tangle and brush of us ready.

How easy to start a fire.
How untrue that ripeness comes only
to the wet and lush.

Telling My Son About His Birth

It was like visiting a house
I'd only seen before between sleep and waking.
I waited days to enter,
but once inside, I was afraid of the dark
and couldn't find the walls.
Maybe there was a storm.
I can't remember, only that I hurt and thought
I wouldn't get out.

I made noises.
Then I found you—
the top of your head black with hair.
I pushed and pushed to get out,
and when we did, into the hot room
where your father and the midwife waited,
I realized I was afraid most
because this house was the world,
and it was on fire.

But you need to know
there wasn't really a house at all
or any shelter. There was a place I cannot name.
You could call it fear or love
or god—it would still be the place
of no place.

Here, there is a real house
made of wood and concrete.
We have names for things
and a name for you.
We think we are past the fire,
asleep in this chair,
your belly on mine
as we breathe on each other.

Jonah and the Tree

You don't say you love that tree but you do.
Are you like this with anything
that gives you food or shade?
Oh, all of you get more rattled
at the sound of my voice in your satiny throats
because you're afraid of how stupid you'll look.

But I come to tell you
compassion always looks stupid
to those well-fed in a shady spot
while time bakes the earth.

Love looks stupid, too
as if the lover had no more sense
than to fling herself into the blank sky
she would soon fall out
like you, Jonah, back to the land
where a tree may mean all
because it makes you the god of it.

But if you lay there long enough
in the rain, you will remember how
the wet ground stretches itself open,
makes earth and sky the inside of a whale,
night unrolling into day,
day unrolling into night
in its old migration
back to me.

Once you can have gone so far,
how can you not let others return?

Swimming in Mombasa at Midnight

I swam on water that must move
to keep its balance,
each stroke of my arms
making the whole pool rush
over itself again.

I swam in the quiet of faint television light
leaking out over the water, the swoosh
of taxis a block away,
while I stared at the moon, asking,
what will it be,
and how will it happen?

Clouds smoked past, a young Kenyan girl
carried the empty Coke bottles
back to the store for us.

And nothing happened. The wind
came and went. The trees paused.
The pool stayed cemented
in the crescent of thick dirt
encased by the Indian ocean.

The earth remained round
so that birds of the next day
could sing as if this life
were almost over,
the next one could now begin.

Hills Climb the Sky

for Laurie

Bill dead a year, I sit in the Mexican restaurant
with Laurie who looks more and more like Bill
crying. So how can he be gone? Laurie in the house
the day after he died, helping me dust c.d. cases.
Laurie in the new house, his picture everywhere, his note
in the recipe box suggesting the garlic dip.
Laurie in his chair, his shirt, and yet all around her
the weather orbits past, outlining how alone she is.

The earth turns on its axis when really
there's no slash of line through the center. Nothing
but fire, rock, underground rivers.
Still, he's not here at each tilt through each anniversary,
each night that rises up from the west while
hills climb the earth in their solitude,
arm in arm with each other yet rolling
alone into shadow.

A year behind the hills, there was a slope of tall grass
where we stood, Bill's ashes all over our fingers
like rain or powder. In the small sway of grass,
60 or so people freezing anyplace we didn't touch,
we spread what was left into the climbing wind
and let the turning of the planet do the rest.

What the Earth Holds

Somewhere Mongols paraded heads on sticks.
Blood moved through dirt like rain.
Cambodians, shot in the back,
dove out of their bones.
And Jews in the gas chamber looked up, stunned
for a moment.

These deaths only seem to evaporate.

The massacres charted in history books,
the massacres we don't know of,
drowned children, buried alive old men,
strangers hanging from branches
in the distance, even the private murders of cavemen
shape rocks, feed trees.

Here, for instance, the deep tangle of big bluestem
and switchgrass surely roots through dirt
that once filtered the blood of the Kaw tribe.
Valleys once blanketed with skulls,
all fever trees now. The bones that bleached
into oblivion, the teeth, the shadows staining sidewalks
all dissolved into dirt and dahlias.

The earth holds it all, more than the mind can imagine.
Meanwhile, our own bodies still warm,
all their weight to love because of and despite
all the skin unwrapped in all the mud,
all the green that still comes.

Holly

1.
At my wedding she wore a bulky turtleneck
under her thrift store gown
and opened her throat
so the world could fall out
the center of her song.

No-one with a voice that strong could disappear.
No-one so prickly pear and granite.

2.
When Holly died there was no funeral.
The Christian Scientists had long ago stopped visiting
and praying hard for her to pray her way out.
She still believed.

"How can you stand this?"
I asked her husband two weeks before.
He leaned his head upon the refrigerator and the room
filled with humming.

"I can't."

3.
So many times I hated how you sucked the life
out of every room you entered.
In the toy department of K-Mart
you screamed how could I know anything,
I didn't have kids yet.

We fought into the pool supply section,
this crazed flare that we would never get past. Something
in the stomach, something in the chest.

4.
Ballet that wrecked your knees,
bookshelves made from cinder blocks,
puppet theaters from refrigerator boxes,
the huge god's eye dangling in mobile,
how you wanted to crawl in the closet
and birth your first child alone,
woolen caps you wore even in spring,
homemade ice cream served after
the macrobiotic dinner,
but you were not to be touched.

5.
When the first diagnosis came, when they had to cut
armpit to sternum while the baby drank pumped milk
and the sun floated one day to the next,
when the dozen pine trees you planted the summer before
moved their tentative fingers in the wind,
when the casseroles paraded through, when you let me
sit with you on the bed and look at the stitches
and later hold the baby up against the visible breast,
his little legs kicking lightly
in the ghost breast, when
was this really?

6.
I want to hear the catch
in the voice, the box of a note
that is anything but a box.
I want to stop feeling uncomfortable
with you undead in the room
telling me I hurt you.

I want to know this song that breaks the mouths
of humans.

The Speed of Life

My son shows me all his eight years at once,
his eyes like the studied pattern of a fossil,
his face grown through a tumble of water and air
from when I first saw him open his black eyes.
His eight-year-old self and his just born self,
and earlier, that almost imperceptible feeling
of something like paper unfolding inside me
all at once, time not a rocket from the past to the future,
from here to there, but time tipped over, spilt out
into the field, the grass first breaking the dirt
with a needlepoint of green, the cut shadow of leaf
on rock 158 million years old, the cockroach descended
from the exact model 250 millions years ago,
the meteor dissolved, the wind beaten in and out of lungs
even before there were lungs.

The outer bowl of the earth fitted perfectly
into the inner bowl of the sky,
my son in my hands the first time
all of him at once contained in two palms.

This is the speed life travels,
so fast, so immediate from all directions
that you can look to the stars
in this galaxy or way beyond

on the same imaginary level ceiling of the heavens,
that you can look at the field
and see all the new grass, old rocks, ancient insects
on the same imaginary floor of the earth.

But what is up close, what fills your hands this moment—
that is the only way we have depth perception.
The tapered valley below the ribs,
the rise of eyelash right out into space,
all the distinctions carefully placed here or there
so we can make age out of this earth,
so we can point at something
as if it's not moving.

Caryn Mirriam-Goldberg

Animals in the House

> *And only then, when I have learned enough,*
> *I will go to watch the animals, and let*
> *something of their composure glide*
> *into my limbs; will see my own existence*
> *deep in their eyes ...*
> ~Rainer Maria Rilke,
> translated by Stephen Mitchell

When my best friend died, I ran,
the sidewalk ending, the sidewalk beginning,
the streetlights coming on as I inhaled,
the dark trailing behind me as I exhaled.

I ran like I'd never run before, no resistance of air or muscle,
no places asking me to stop and enter.

That rhythmic landing and leaving again, the slight bumps
of small pebble or curb actually sped me up.
No longer afraid of hurting myself or getting lost.
Nothing but the lust for speed.

I ran because this is what animals in pain do.

❖ ❖ ❖

I light the shiva candle, the white wax filling
the glass cylinder, and now a flame to tell me
my father was alive, my father is dead.

As if fire can make sense out of running water
like a fever that smears all the dreams into static.
I hold this candle and read the Braille of the heart.
An animal who has lost its way. A territory so new
I first have to grow eyes to see it.

❖ ❖ ❖

We lie in bed and kiss, the kitten perched
dangerously by our heads, claws extended,

the happy dog hopelessly crying
because he's so in love with what hates him,
the loose redbird crashing into the window
again, and all the animals, microscopic,
all over the houses of our bodies.

I put my mouth on your mouth,
all the bones so well hidden under
these kisses. Your palms on my shoulders,
my thighs wrapped around your legs, the indentations
we make on the mattress, everything falling
toward another core of gravity
within the core of the earth. Which is
the man, which the woman? Who speaks
Spanish or Japanese in the next room?
I can't remember what we're doing
anymore. Water in water.
Animals circled around
the empty place in the field.

❖ ❖ ❖

Each night, it's the dream of another house.
The room below the basement I never noticed before,
and at its most interior, a whole slew of rooms,
empty and lit, some even with balconies
overlooking underground rivers.

Sometimes, it's a small place—a third-story apartment.
Or a single room suspended in the woods,
hard to find except in winter when the openness
of the trees surprises us. One house is full of
horses instead of furniture, panthers instead of dogs.

When the doctor says, "you have cancer,"
I take notes carefully, amazed
at the smoothness of the pen on paper
when the ground dissolves,
the falling begins and doesn't end.

Just a small mutation, a creature growing
out of bounds. Cancer,
I say aloud, on the phone, into the quiet air
that surrounds me just before sleep,
as if I'm naming a house so horizontal
it's impossible to ever blueprint.

The losses mounting as the wheel
of the world turns day to night,
night to day, a childhood cardboard cutout,
the ways stars fan over us just so.
In the dark, the lightning bug caught
in the curtain. In the light, the baby
batting at floating dusk, laughing.

How many losses do you know?

The bear dead in its cave. The root
of wild onion sliced by the shovel
where we'll plant wild onion.
The larkspur no one human sees.
The rain frogs lose to tree roots under puddles.
How many lost animals climb the darkness?

I've thrown myself down for a life
and I would do it again,
not out of nobility or love
but because I can't help it.

Animals fold themselves into sleep,
give their breath to their young without knowing
anything but the heat under fur,
in the heart beating, and between each beat,
the open fields where anything can happen.

I fell into that animal world,
and couldn't leave without first pushing
that first child out of me, my whole life
thrown against the light like a shadow.
All the sounds of one chase
or another, all the caught animals
taking air into themselves,
making it theirs, letting it go.

Spring Song

What is it to wake at night not watered down
in overdrawn voices from the day, to see the space
and not the figure in the space, to fall backwards
in a dream and realize it's a dream?
What waits, wet as fire, on the end of the line?
The rushing of wings, the billowing of thunderheads,
the crashing of car into lamp post, the slivering of bark
from tree, the waking suddenly for no reason?

Meanwhile, insects reproduce themselves like breath,
birds loosen the sky with flight,
stratus clouds streak across the moon,
kisses stop, and stones break apart
so easily that it's clear they've been cracked inside
for a long time. Each life a transference of water.
Each act just a way to move light around.

Even knowing this, why can't the heart stop asking?

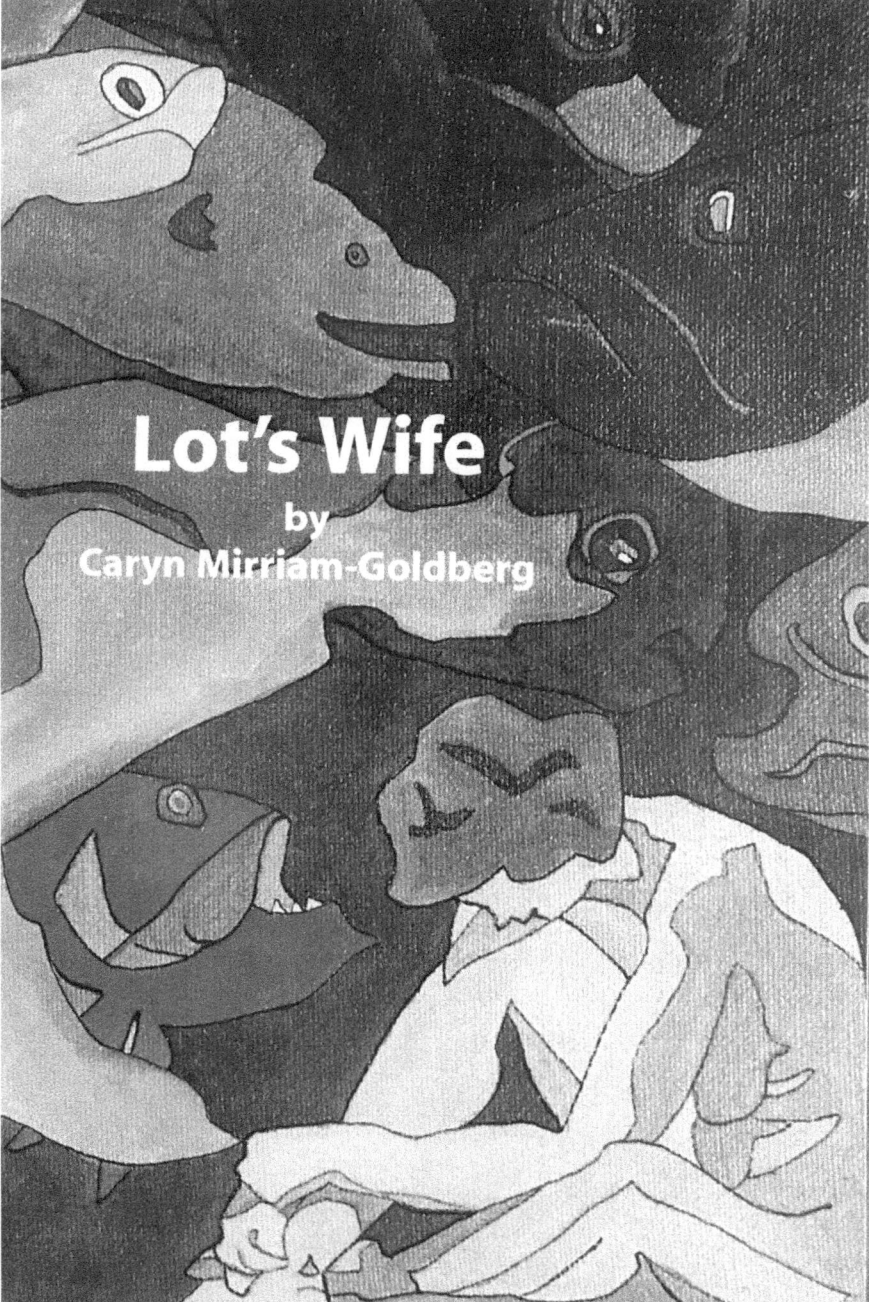

The Mortician's Daughter

How much lives in scraps.
So I hold tight to the laundry of the dead
as my dad stretches open their eyes
so everyone can see them
almost asleep.

He hides the signs—the marks
on ankles or wrists, the tiny scars
while I blend the skin colors into their faces.
I don't mind.

Sometimes we take gold from a tooth,
or a heavy stoned ring off a finger
right before the final closing of the lid.
Who's to know? my father says.
So I drop these things into my pocket,
later fish them out on the kitchen table
where my father waits
right before bed.

But I don't go to bed.
I sit on the crate in the backyard
in moon or cloud light,
no longer breathing the same air
left over by the bodies or my father.
I eat some clover, watch the starlings fall
up the trees with their new-found food.
Nothing's a weed—look at me—the invisible girl
behind the dumpster in the alley.

Look at the birds—
so smart to eat the edges of bread!
That's where the fire leaves its streak,
that's what tastes best.

Imaginary Friend

I lie with you at twilight
and say, it's okay, you still have me
holding you on the bed
behind the door that no one opens.
You make up a story about a girl
who wouldn't eat lamb chops and
a dog that would. She gets caught
but escapes and drives the car to Mexico
even if she can't drive yet.

But I know what really happened,
how your father told you to turn,
lean your hands on the counter
while he took off his belt and snapped it.

You make up stories all your life,
like when the girl walked too slowly
one morning and her father kicked her over,
then said, get up, get to work.

What's so terrible about that,
you ask me. What's so bad about bruises
everywhere in the blue light
of almost dark when we're together?
I'm here with you. I don't give up.
Even if one morning you wake, forgetting
how I watch for where you step,
and open the door to the blaze of sky
everywhere—all walls and roof gone,
men with hammers taking apart the house
because your father wants it built another way.
Even when you're older and sitting in the hospital
with your hand through the opening
of the isolette to touch your son
you want but aren't allowed to hold yet.

Caryn Mirriam-Goldberg

I wait for you your whole life,
not something you made up,
but air against air, light against light
draped over your shoulders
like a sweater of no weight.

The Bad Monster Contemplates Her Badness from a Lounge Chair at K-Mart

I want to drop everything I hold:
infants with delicate long fingers, light bulbs,
anything made of glass or pastry
not to mention older children who run to me, lift
their arms to the sky and say, tell me
about riding in space shuttles and eating
parking meters, tell me how you walked
across the face of a crying person and didn't care.

I'm not stupid. I don't tell them a thing.
I make little cathedrals out of popsicle sticks
that people like because a monster made them
and that must prove something.

I go to a lot of psychologists
who act like they're not afraid, even
when I claw their cute little business cards
and matching pillows.
I can't help it, I tell them
in my nicely-pressed hair
while the worms inside hollow out
the vaults of my wanting to be nice as pudding.
I want people to love me
not out of pity or projection anymore.
I want to be the good monster
bundling flowers together for the blind,
nursing crack babies in the dark
and singing the sweetest song
they'll never hear.

But I'm still the bad monster, exhausted
on this lounge chair in K-Mart, just waiting
for someone to recognize me in my hideous sleep
and kiss me good.

Hagar on the Mountain

I climb to the sound
of javelinas eating cactus.
In the path a kit fox stops,
looks up, afraid I would try
to touch. I bend slowly
to lower our son to the rocks.
No fox. Microscopic insects
sleep in my sweat.

The boy wakes and asks why
we do not build a fire big enough
for Abraham to find us.
I lift him and let his head
weigh against the bone
of my shoulder. At the top field
wind rises. Our voices rust
in the thinning air.

I will carry him all night
if I must, my son's whisper songs
telling me how the water
falls over the side of rock,
my hand on his forearm,
promising something.

A place to stop, a well
surrounded by animals
where we'll learn to dream God's dream
like all the others.

Rapunzel in the Desert

Once a torrent of hair led him up to me.
I was frightened at first. He was much taller
than the witch, but soon he hummed into my hair
on the pillow as streaks of moonlight moved
on his arched back.
I gave him an egg and said it was my promise.
When it hatched, wishes would rise like naked chicks,
and I would come to him.

The witch found the egg
missing and cut me
from my hair. She tied her scarf around
my eyes and took me for a long ride.
I woke in this desert with a flock of chickens,
a barrel of apples.
The chickens live on tiny worms and cores.
Each day I make a hole in egg and drink.

At night I sleep in the white grass,
the dark so clear I can see the moon turn,
and dream of a blind man below my tower,
tapping the stone walk for me.

When, once each winter, it rains,
the chickens hide under the brush.
I stand outside and let the drops
beat the dust from my palms.

The Snow Queen

Of course I'm cold, I'm freezing
and can't touch myself, can't
look in mirrors or skim
warm soup with my forefinger.

Look at me, drowning
in this thin air.
The white furs do no good.
Neither does the down
nor comb-carved horses.
I'm sick of living here,
pretending to love little boys
or despise little girls.
I'm tired of all the petty wars
staged in my honor,
and all the babes I left
frozen from bad milk
in their white gowns
and crinkled eyelids.

The warm-blooded wolves snicker
at the chiming icicles
across my forehead
while the weather glides past
stagnant as glaciers.

Just let me turn into a woman fat
with wrinkles and cream,
living well so far away
in such an orchard of green apples.

The Woman Who Cannot Feel

She must do everything by mirror, her brain singed
by some electric stream that cleared
all trails of feeling.
She tells her reflection of hands
to clasp the hook and eye
of the bra behind her back.
She orders the muscles in her face
to tense or relax, watching them obey.
Sometimes she finds bruises
on her arm or notices her left foot
turning out as she walks,
her body no longer able
to lead itself blindly along the path
in the woods or turn away from the corner
of a table buried in the flesh
of her hip.

When she makes love, she watches
him closer, his eyes closed, closing
tighter, his hard breath like a room
that captures her, makes her wait
blind and deaf until
he can move back, let her
see the softer lines in his forehead,
let her hear her name.

Three Women With Breast Cancer

One had the oranges in her breasts cut out,
and then, by slight of hand or wink, a new orange
appeared in her brain. She thought she had demons,
but people said, you're probably just depressed.

Another had breasts bigger than honeydew,
so big that after the surgeons carved them off
she kept falling backwards.
Now she shops with weights on her chest
while secret fruit grows in her head and sternum.

The third let them slice armpit
to nipple, taking the black walnut away.
She won't go for x-rays or biopsies anymore
but she hobbles, she coughs.
She tries to see herself a tall, thick trunk
with leaves so green I'm blinded
when I look up through her.
What if a plum grows in her lungs
or a peach pit already gathers thoughts to itself
behind her eyes?

I want to know where this fruit falls from.
What kind of tree would do this to a woman?
A tree of air and dirt? A tree of blood,
its canopy spreading like spilled water
into the sky? Meanwhile, these women walk,
their heads so close to the forest's understory,
their feet on the ground where light bleeds
at regular intervals, and all around
the knots of bone and branch loosen.

Inside the Wolf

It happens all the time in fairy tales.
The women offer up their lives willingly,
with pain but no second thoughts.
The mermaid trades her voice for three days
of human legs. The grandmother enters the wolf's mouth.

I know how it works: the mermaid fails
and throws herself into the sea
because this is the rule.
The grandmother doesn't dream
of rescue. Then the surprise: angels
lift her from the foam or she wakes to the tip
of the huntsman's knife.

I sit on the bed in daylight and try to breathe
or not be disturbed by how the baby
compresses my lungs. Soon he'll drop
toward the outside world, and I'll try
to lie down without swimming, without floating
while the waves rush over my face
in slow motion. Having done this before
won't help. The body forgets so quickly
how to give up, close its eyes,
stop thinking.

But afterwards I'll lie down—breathless,
the baby's hand on my collarbone—
in the shaking of one who's been pulled
from the wolf, just in time,
but doesn't know it.

Psyche

He puts his hand on my shoulder.
Lifts it but it's still there.
Then the wings take away
the face I'm not to see.

I lie on the mat as morning floats
rectangles of light across the floor.
Almost asleep, I remember
a gold bowl on the shelf with scenes
of a dancer shading his eyes,
lacquered boxes being carried up
by a veiled woman to the mouth of a cave,
ants separating grain, even a woman
plunging into a river at night
to swim toward sheep.

When I look up I see
no gold bowl. A blank wall of white.
Blue curtains and the shadows
counting their ways past.

Tonight, I'll bring a lamp
to stare astonished at him,
to see if his hair is like waves.
I'll want to touch him
but the oil will land first
on his shoulder and wake us
into a current like sound,
into a voice piercing bone.

Circe Bawls Out An Aging Snow White

Why do you come here? What do you want
from me? Those dwarves, they're no good,
not like dogs. Dogs are the best way
for men to go, it keeps them
honest, underfoot, faithful as fur.

You lay dead in that box.
You know what I'm talking about.
How did you expect life to be after 60?
That prince isn't half as good
as one of your damn dwarves
who don't know enough to die
when they get old.

So you paddle to my island, ask why
I gave you that poison comb
and bustle. As if I cared
about being beautiful, as if jealousy
were as strong a motive as boredom.
I told you I can't turn old women
into anything good.

Sit down and eat these crackers,
and I'll tell you where the bones in your feet go
when the poison weighs down to the extremities.
It's how most of you die, cancer or bad breath,
Something that turns you into a heavy rope
of bones someone must carry
to the commode. It's how the mind goes,
unable to believe anymore
in its own desirability.

You don't want to die?
Then you must change something
behind you. Live with the filth of dogs,
smear the beautiful woodwork of the castle
with your fingerprints. Live like me on the bones
of what you thought you could love.

Caryn Mirriam-Goldberg

Lazarus's Wife

Enough already! Widow, wife, widow,
wife, I hardly know what
to wear most days.

When I come home, there he is—
stretched out on the couch
with a beer in his hand, the other cans
strewn empty on the floor.
"It's almost worth coming back,"
he says. Then belches.

Everyone was surprised the first time
but after the third funeral
they stopped coming and now want
the casserole pans back
for once and for good.

I can't blame them.
The dead who don't stay dead
ruin everything—
the carpet, for instance,
and the lace coverlet.

Nothing so bad except for the stress
of having so much to clean
and knowing he didn't do this for me.

The Woman Who Saved Moses

She often stared at the fast river
after she lost the baby. Illegitimate,
her father, the Pharoah, said, better you bleed
for a month than I send it to its grave later.

Afterward, she went each day to the same water
that distilled the blood her servants rinsed
from her underclothes, the same water
she had floated in all her life.

No longer entering it, she watched
how the Nile distorted ripples
made by insects, or the reflection
of her face and tree branches
in its speed.

One afternoon the basket with the baby came,
clear and certain. She dove,
her arms and legs weighted against
the current to save him.

What could her father say now that the gods
sent proof she must have the child?

Every day since, she kneels in the mud to drink
from the Nile's mouth, praying,
as one would for rain during a drought,
that the blood in her body turns to milk.

Demeter Is Persephone

There were never two women, just me
split in two, down the middle
as if I'd been struck by lightning.

"Put your young self underground,"
Zeus said. "Keep it safe there
from your bitter half."
As if being a mother erased
all the sweetness,

all the hazelnuts ground
and pressed, all the gourds
hollowing on the windowsill in winter.
As if all that's harvested
has no choice but to dry out,
grow an aftertaste.

I've got the first taste fresh
on my tongue, my life as a daughter
who wanted to give herself completely
to the fields of corn, bordered
in clover and sweetgrass.
I know what it is to twirl
in the loose gauze skirt,
then lie shaded on my mother's lap
and eat white cherries together,
oblivious to how rare
this would seem later.

And I know how my body
would actually split,
so she could come out of me
and we could stare at each other,
a whole animal in its strong skin
long before they put her on the inside
of the tree, pressing out;
me on the outside, imbedding the pattern of bark
into the mirror of my skin.

Song of Songs

> *Who is this that cometh up out of*
> *the wilderness*
> *like pillars of smoke?*
> *~ Song of Songs*

This is the song of songs we sing—
a circle of women on the grass and dirt
some place where no gardens dwell.

This is the song inside the song
of *he raped me*, or a little louder,
I'm shaking, I'm also learning to knit,
her eyelashes landing on her cheek.
The song of *I wasn't wanted*,
and *I was wanted so much*
he cut a star on my stomach.

This is the inside song no one hums later,
a song in four parts, made of the air
right before rain as well as the air
streaking and not gleaming
in the hardest of rain.
We sit on the ground and say things
we cannot say without breaking.
This could have happened,

could be happening as we speak
or don't speak. Ten of us, thirty-six of us,
seventy-one of us lying face down in the grass, alive.
Which one lost the baby, which one killed
her beaded heart, which one fell in love and made
a pot of barley soup? Meanwhile, the wind
sings grass as it always has, the dirt expands

all winter long, the stones shift under us
singing from the inside out
in the slowest of motion.
No smoke. No pillars anymore.

Come. Hold this stone in your palm
and sing the song of songs
with your roundest of words.

Lot's Wife

Why "not look back"?
Why "salt"? I stand in the desert
and lick my fingers. So salty
even though it's a place
ordinary people shouldn't sweat,

but I'm not ordinary—I'm a pillar,
suspended on the banks of what was bad
and what was an escape.
"Why look back?" the vulture asks.
"Why not go with the kids
to that new salvation?"

Instead, I'm frozen here, cactus-like,
remembering the songs trained
to follow me my whole life.
I didn't go with them.
I looked back into the center
of the bodies rushing like water
and saw something ringed
with blood and salt:
a thumb print deeply imbedded on the world.

I looked quickly into my own imagination of the past
and believed this was solid ground
after oceans recede.

But the way salt
clings to salt, hardens
in the sun, it hurts me sometimes.
It makes me want to stop remembering.

The Grandmother in the Mental Hospital

She used to hide things: pliers
in the refrigerator, a roll of stamps
behind the canister of flour.
This drove my father crazy
but I liked it: opening drawers
and seeing things you never expected together.

Now she lies on the narrow bed
while the baby pushes her wheelchair.
Let him, she says, staring
at her quiet lamp. I tell her
about his new sneakers and the weather
until she waves to me to be quiet.
I don't like how her room faces
another building. And all the pills
that don't work, that never have,

and I don't like how my father, 25 years ago,
would gladly hold open the door of the Buick
to drive her here so she could sign in
the crooked letters of her name and cry
when they said more shock therapy was a good idea.

"I'm going to die," she says,
but she has always said that.
Always, stories of potato fields
where her good brothers and sister
should have been buried instead of in mass graves;
the way we ate too much
or too little, the lost son, the too-small
apartment, the stupid neighbors, the bad weather
and what they did to her mother in Poland.

She sits up and falls into me.
"I never thought it would be like this,"

but how else could it be?
She lets me hold her, takes my hand
that two months from now will take the shovel
from my mother to push another clump of dirt
into her grave where all the crazy things,
finally quiet, fall together.

Eve in Northeastern Australia

I am alone but not in danger.
That is, I think I am safe
even with Adam, who cursed this red ground,
gone to find some place blindingly holy.

On my knees in the cradle of the Baobab tree,
I light the shabbat candles,
shielding the flame from fragments
of wind. Everywhere there's kiwi
to suck the pulp from,
one dog in the blue distance,

and my twin sons crying in the cave
off and on in the carnage of the wind.
I will go to them but first
I sing this prayer of light,
first I circle my hands
in the blurred air of the flame
and speak to fire:

I will shield you from God
with my good hands.
We will be safe here.
You, my twin of wax.
Me, your mirror of bone.

Eurydice

The truth is I rose
quickly into the face of the sky, into the rain
knocking away dust and feathers
from my secret mind.

I rose out of long grass and smooth leaves
too light for air to hold,
right out of his arms
the first time,
right out of his sight
the second.

This underground scenario is his story, his way
of saying he's better than me,
that it was all his choice
whether we kissed eye to eye
or just in memory.

It's not that I don't miss him
or the smell of dirt
in the crevices of petals.
But the air—it's a secret
that keeps promising to tell itself,
a drumming on my body
of wind and sun, a rush upward
past the upsidedown world
to the divide of sky and space—
where stars fall all night
through my floating hair
and the dark opens
its singing mouth to me

Caryn Mirriam-Goldberg

Moses's Sister

I watch him all my life.
"Make sure he lives,"
mother says. "Make sure."

I'd rather watch deer
just before dark
or rabbits in the sand
where they don't belong.
They're not so predictable.

My brother wants the weight
of people watching
to prove he's making a dent
in the air.

He wants to talk to god,
then tell everyone god is
a burning thing
stuck in the ground.
But I know better.
God is a watching thing
that can't be seen.

What burns is only the wanting to see.

Leah

You sit on the ridge alone at dusk watching
the mist swim the valley in hush,
occasional deer along the tree line.
The night pours up from the earth in blue black.
This is when you listen best,
let fall a handful of dirt,
a whole planet, back to itself.

Nothing is what it seems with Jacob, with Rachel
but here, the center of each tree leads,
ring by ring, back to an acorn,
a handful of dirt orbiting
in heat and dark and rain
like your own life ringed
with pain, ringed with stories
of falling or being pushed
into the ground
where the smell of god
bears down on you.

Here, lie down, bury half your face
in the earth, the other half
in the bath of air. And when
you are ready, turn completely
into the dirt and let the first sound
you make reach the stones
hot underground from where
the earth heats itself.

Cinderella's Mother as Hazel Tree

See my daughter sit and cry
right under my lowest branches?
I lower balloons of leaf
trying to convince her
I'm not dead,
even drop a switch
she could use on her father
if she'd just open her eyes.

If she would only look at me
she might understand
how to hold light in an upsidedown fan—
a tease of broad green
in half circles, sun bleeding
everywhere in our heads.

Then she could see
my trunk grown smooth over where it once split,
my egg-shaped leaves red at the center vein,
and all the new branches brown and slim
as her young wrist.

If I could speak in words, I'd tell her
how such a transformation took place,
how even my roots will outlive
all the evil, all the fear.

But I'm not the paper they'll make for her fairy tale.
I'm what the paper, left outside long enough,
will return to.

Mirrors

The queen had a magic mirror
in which she could see
even the grain of the apple
as it approached Snow White's
open mouth, the juice released
upon her lips as she lay
quietly in the glass case.

The prince saw his own reflection
and kissed, releasing himself
to a mirror that deceived
like the lighted mirrors women sit before
in their slips, preparing their faces
like surgeons. It lied like the mirrors
of high-school locker rooms
that show the astonished faces
of girls undressing the white quarters
of their bodies in the light
of each others' scared eyes.

When Snow White sat up, the queen
broke the mirror with her fist,
the lines of blood curling
around her hand, her pulse
beating like the approaching horses
of the prince and his lover,
awakened into a mirror of revenge.

The queen could never see herself
in her mirror, only what she hated.
Years after she tumbled from the kingdom,
she found her reflection in a pond
and could not believe how her beauty
reversed itself through ugliness,
back to a beauty that told only

of the sway of tall oaks,
the scuttle of deer away
from her approach, the twist
of clouds into rain
that streaked the dust on her cheeks.

Telling My Daughter About Her Birth

I would have left my body
if leaving hadn't meant not returning.
I would have climbed my bones to the ceiling
and watched, remarking, ah, look
at that screaming woman. She'll be fine
in an hour or two.

But I stayed, tried to lie down
without the panic and bargaining
of one who'd do anything not to feel the pain.
I yelled: I give up. I yelled back: no, I don't.
I screamed the peacock scream, the scared woman scream,
the bear, the broken-record screams. I stood up
and sat down, stood up and sat down
as if I wasn't in a room, or I was the whole room
and could change the shape of it by lifting my arm,

could change the certainty of the air outside
crashing through the ceiling with its new weight,
my body cracked open like a plum,
and at the center, like at the center of a rock or planet,
something shimmering, sealed
around its bones.

I stood up and felt that hot round thing,
a head, a ball of body,
a skull, a planet, an egg
suspended, one ball slipping out
of another in eclipse, the metallic sheen
of everything,

and a split second later
the light, the dark outside, returned
and I was holding you.
I was holding you
as you opened your eyes

I Love You

I love you without knowing what it means
no matter how many trees climb uselessly,
the clouds dangerous in their sheen.
I love you stupid as any tree thinking
the grass is useless, the sky background
noise, the sprinkler a god, the wide mouthed lake
a mirror to leave and never return to.

I let myself fall on the bed slow motion
because I love you without knowing anything
about how this fall will take my whole life.
The earth fixed in orbit. Your hands climb me
in surprise, a trellis made of bones.
Everything between us like weather
that is never about destination but dropping intent.

Do you know how many times
I've stared at the curve of your cheekbone
thinking this has nothing to do with me?
But as soon as your eyes notice, the walls
of the room fall slow motion out all directions
we're holding each other without touching
or touching. I'm trying to look at you in the dark
that isn't the negation of space but a shaping thing—
a way to unspill color back to whatever we were
before this body or after. Just beyond your lips,
the teeth guarding the skull that will survive you.
I love your skin replacing itself at the speed of light spent
through window panes on this slate of daylight,
where I cannot stop saying,

I love you blind. I love you long.
I love you over the crest of the water
the air the babies the branches
walking beneath birds

to will into being by loving away the will.
I love you halfway up the life where we lay
body doubles for how well we'd love
if the body was about
to turn back to wind.

I stop climbing
and say I love you glistening
with one of the million slivers of the evil mirror
imbedded in my heart. I love you
from the bottom of my smashed mirror.
Don't you see, nothing is impenetrable?

Acknowledgments

I'm very grateful to:

- All who have held lanterns along the meandering fields and woods of the writing life, including members of the Wakarusa Nine and other writing groups: Denise Low, Judy Roitman, Kelley Hunt, Harriet Lerner, Stan Lombardo, Ken Irby, Karen Ohnesorge, Roy Beckemeyer, Victoria Sherry, Jim McCrary, Kat Greene, Holly Exner, Sally McNall, Mary Klayder, Reva Friedman, and Erleen Christensen.
- The many teachers I studied with along the way: William Stafford, Roy Gridley, Chester Sullivan, Mike Johnson, Howard Levy, Beth Schultz, Anne Waldman, Jane Kenyon, Stanley Plumley, Brenda Hillman, Galway Kinnell, Sharon Olds, Yusef Komunakyaa, Carolyn Doty, Victor Contoski, and others.
- Stephen Locke, my co-author, the photographer who inspired many of the poems in *Chasing Weather: Tornadoes, Tempest, and Thunderous Skies in Word and Image*.
- Fellow Kansas poets laureate Denise Low, Wyatt Townley, Eric McHenry, Jonathan Holden, Kevin Rabas, and Huascar Medina, who all shone light wide and high while traveling deep across and beyond Kansas.
- My publishers for all previous collections of poetry: Ice Cube Press with Steve Semken, Spartan Press with Jason Ryberg, Mammoth Press with Denise Low, Woodley Memorial Press with Kevin Rabas, Bob Lawson, and Amy Fleury.
- Tracy Million Simmons of Meadowlark Books for her grace, patience, art, and passion for this book and many others by Midwestern writers. Big thanks to Linda Lassman for proofreading the new poems.
- Daniel, Natalie, and Forest, our kids who gave me ample material to write about and didn't mind too much when I vanished into poems and fed them pizza for dinner instead.
- Hugs to my cover artists: Celia Smith (*Lot's Wife*), Paul Hotvedt (*Animals in the House*), Kathy Hird Wright (*Reading the Body*), Teri Evans (*Landed*), Stephen Locke (*Chasing Weather*), and Rodney Troth (*Following the Curve*).
- Ken Lassman, love of my life, and first and last audience for all my poems (not to mention the source of lots of good ideas for poems). You're the most embodied poem I read.

Source Notes:

Many poems in *Following the Curve* draw from yoga asanas (poses) with the Sanskrit name following the English translation as well as the Yamas and Niyamas which, with the Asanas, are part of the eight branches of Yoga practice and theory. Big hugs to my main yoga teachers: Anne Underwood and Gopi Sandal, and others I studied with: Laura Ramberg, MariaAna Garza, Rita York, and Anna Guest-Jelley.

"What the Ocean Can Know of a Body" (lines in italics) draws from Dar Williams's song, "The Ocean," used with permission.

"Your Life is Your Life" steals its title from a line in Charles Bukowski's "The Laughing Heart."

"I Want to Tell You How Beautiful You Are" draws from the first line of River Malcolm's "Every Woman Deserves a poem."

"This is Not the Easy Poem to Write" was written using a prompt of the same title in a workshop led by Seema Reza at Goddard College.

Many of the poems in *Lot's Wife* (and some other collections too) riff off biblical stories, myths, and fairy tales, including "I Love," drawing from Hans Christian Anderson's "The Snow Queen."

"Gateway" riffs off the *Tao Te Ching*, translated by Stephen Mitchell.

"Just-Doing-That-Moon" is the name of the month of March according to the Osage tribe that once occupied Kansas, Missouri, Oklahoma, and Arkansas.

"Havdalah," refers to the Havdalah service, which begins at sundown on Saturday to mark the end of the sabbath. It is a short service invoking the senses—a braided candle, a spice box, a cup of wine, singing, holding each other—to welcome the new week.

Publication Acknowledgments:

150 Kansas Poems, poem of the week, edited by Julie Ramon: "Mercy. Courage. Daring," and edited by Laura Lee Washburn: "Body of Time."

5 A.M.: "Lazarus' Wife."

Alaska Poetry Review: "Holly."

An Endless Skyway: Poetry from the State Poets Laureate of America, edited by Denise Low, Marilyn L. Taylor, Walter Bargen, and Caryn Mirriam-Goldberg: "The Dreaming Land," "Just-Doing-That Moon," "Downward Dog," "Self-Portrait as Pond," "In the End, There is Only Kindness," Self-Portrait as Grown-Up," and "The Last Moment."

Bards Against Hunger, edited by Kevin Rabas: "The Wish," "You Are Not Alone," and "Permission."

Begin Again: 150 Kansas Poems, edited by Caryn Mirriam-Goldberg: "Celebrate This Kansas" and "Magnolia Tree in Kansas."

Black Spring: "What Would Happen If You Walked Here?"

California Quarterly: "Lightning, No Thunder."

The Carbon Chronicles, edited by Matthew Fowler: "Lazarus's Wife" and "Telling My Daughter About her Birth."

Cincinnati Poetry Review: "Rapunzel in the Desert," first place (best of issue).

Communities Magazine: "Song of Songs."

Connotations: "The Life You Could Be Living (If You Weren't Living This One)," "Questions for Home," "The Last Moment," "Advice for the Material World," "Self-Portrait as Grown-Up."

Cordella: "The Midrash of the Heart" and "Shabbat."

Ekphrasis: "Hold to the Center" and "The World Says."

Examined Life: "What the Mostly Blind Eye Sees"

The Exquisite Corpse: "About Desire."

First Intensity: "Self-Portrait as Boddhisatva," "Self-Portrait Before Birth," "Self-Portrait at Two and a Half," and "Self-Portrait as Fuckhead."

Flint Hills Review: "When the Train Stops in Brooklyn," "Who Dances?" "You Are Never Alone," and "When the Sun is Closest to the Earth."

Futures Trading: "After the Storm, the Stars," "Finding the Moon," "When Her Work is Done, she forgets it/ That is why it lasts forever."

George Washington Review: "Girl."

Harbor Review: "What Happens in the Dark."

Higginson Review: "Leap."

I-70 Review: "The Light In Between."

Imagination and Place, edited by Laurie Ward and Rick Mitchell: "Self-Portrait as River of Starlings."

Inkwell Journal: "So Much is Other Than It Could Be"

Journey Daily with a Compelling Poem Podcast: "All Those Birds Flying Off That Tree" and "Celebrate This Kansas."

Kansas Audubon: "Celebrate This Kansas."

Kansas City Star: "Spring Song."

Kansas City Voices: "Self-Portrait as Ecstasy."

Kaw: A Spoken Word CD: "Girl."

Kansas City Studio: "Self-Portrait as Wind."

Laurel Review: "Demeter Is Persephone."

Lawrence Journal-World: "Self-Portrait As Woman Who Loves Her Body for a Moment," "Self-Portrait as Wind," "Magnolia Tree in Kansas" and "Spring Song."

Little Balkans Review: "Lullaby for the Changing Moon," "Lost," "Migration of Animals," "Let the Rivers Clap Their Hands," and "The Door of the Grass."

Lilith: "The Grandmother in the Mental Hospital."

The Literary Review: "Tricks of Gravity."

Louisville Review: "Eurydice."

Lucy Writers: "Copeland Falls," "Prevernal," and "Under the 400-Year-Old Ponderosa Pine."

Lullwater Review: "Happiness."

Midwest Quarterly: "Writing in the Field," "Landed," "Field," "The Coldest Night," and "Hold to the Center."

Minnesota Review: "Telling My Son About His Birth."

Mizmor Anthology: "The Sound of the Big Thompson"

Mothering: "Telling My Son About His Birth."

Mocking Heart Review: "Crossing Over," "Jericho," "God in the Trees," "The Last Light of the Year," and "Visitor" (featured poet for issue).

The Moon Anthology, edited by Sue Brannan Walker and Philip Colin: "When the Moon Opened My Life."

Negative Capability: "The People Who Pose In Front of Monet's Water Lilies," "No One Tells You What to Expect," "All Those Birds Flying Off That Tree," and "The Opposite of Certainty" (featured poet for issue).

New Laurel Review: "The People Who Wanted to Steal You."

New Letters: "Thresholds."

New Mexico Poetry Review: "When the Rain Comes" and "Winter Solstice: 4:22 p.m."

The New Territory: "Being Made of Weather"

Nimrod: "Between Air and Water."

Phoebe: "The Grandmother in the Mental Hospital."

The Phoenix Papers, edited by Stephen Addis and Stanley Lombardo: "Animals in the House" and "About Desire."

Planet Drum Pulse: "Coordinates."

Poetry Bay: "How Time Moves," "In Transit," and "Prevernal."

Poets & Writers: "The Language of Art."

A Ritual to Read Together: Poems in Conversation with William Stafford: "Talking to Stafford Late at Night."

River City Poetry: "No One Tells You What to Expect," "All I Have Lost to February," "Everything That Rises," "We Have Prepared For This All Our Lives," and "Your Grief for What You've Lost."

The Shining Years, edited by Gary Lechliter: "The Gone Ones" and "Time Names Its Age."

Sojourner: "Moses' Sister."

Somewhere Between Kansas City and Denver, edited by Jason Ryberg: "Getting Started," "The Yoga of Memory" and "Finding the Fire (Tapas)."

Song of Eretz: "Inscription," "Riding Backwards Through Childhood," "Gateway," "Almost Gone," and "Who Dances?"

South Dakota Review: "Hagar on the Mountain."

Tar River Poetry Review: "The Woman Who Cannot Feel."

Terrain: "What the Sky is Made Of" and "You Rise Up to Meet the Falling World."

To the Stars Through Difficulties: A Kansas Renga in 150 Voices, edited by Caryn Mirriam-Goldberg: "No Other Way."

Typishly: "Entering the Days of Awe."

Visions International: "Three Women With Breast Cancer."

Voice of the Turtlee: "That Tree is a Genius."

Willow Springs: "Jonah and the Tree" and "The Snow Queen."

Wind: "The Mortician's Daughter."

WomenSpirit: "When the Train Stops in Brooklyn."

Writing Out of Time: "After the Winter of No Winter."

Xanadu: "Eve in Northwest Australia."

Zingara Poetry: "Valentine."

About the Photographer

Photographer and artist Tony Peterson explains, "My work doesn't fit neatly into any particular category, however the nature of structures and the structures of nature are a common theme. The focus is often on particular elements of light, pattern, or color rather than a documentation of the object or scene itself. Periodically when I'm drawn to a subject I'm not entirely sure at the moment what attracted me. It's only after I've photographed it that my eyes can see what my mind did. Consequently much of my photography has to be visually explored because there are often elements not immediately obvious."

A native of Little River, Peterson moved to Lawrence in 1982 to attend KU. After earning a degree in Journalism he worked in the non-profit and human service field for 25 years before returning to his lifelong interest in art and photography.

About the Author

Caryn Mirriam-Goldberg, Ph.D., the 2009-13 Kansas Poet Laureate is the author of two dozen books including *Miriam's Well* (a novel), *Everyday Magic: A Field Guide to the Mundane and Miraculous*, *The Sky Begins At Your Feet: A Memoir on Cancer, Community, and Coming Home to the Body*, and *Following the Curve*, poetry. A teacher for the Transformative Language Arts Network, she offers online classes, coaches people on writing and right livelihood through the arts, and consults with businesses and organizations on creativity.

DaveLeikerPhotography.com

Caryn facilitates Brave Voice: Writing & Singing for Your Life retreats, workshops, and performances with singer Kelley Hunt, and she leads Your Right Livelihood, a training on doing the work you love, with storyteller Laura Packer. She is also a roving scholar for Humanities Kansas and the Osher Institute. A teacher for the Transformative Language Arts Network, she offers online classes in writing for vitality and discovery, and facilitation for community and change.

Caryn makes her home with her husband, bioregional writer Ken Lassman, in the country south of Lawrence, Kansas, where they restore tallgrass prairie and try to keep up with dogs, cats, and visiting adult children. She writes often on the porch, immersed in wind and birdsong.

www.CarynMirriamGoldberg.com

WWW.MEADOWLARK-BOOKS.COM

Nothing feels better than home

meadowlark-books.com

While we at Meadowlark Books love to travel, we also cherish our home time. We are nourished by our open prairies, our enormous skies, community, family, and friends. We are rooted in this land, and that is why Meadowlark Books publishes regional authors.

When you open one of our fiction books, you'll read delicious stories that are set in the Heartland. Settle in with a volume of poetry, and you'll remember just how much you love this place too—the landscape, its skies, the people.

Meadowlark Books publishes memoir, poetry, short stories, and novels. Read stories that began in the Heartland, that were written here. Add to your Meadowlark Book collection today.

Specializing in Books by Authors from the Heartland Since 2014

www.ingramcontent.com/pod-product-compliance
Lightning Source LLC
Chambersburg PA
CBHW022100150426
43195CB00008B/206